Invest in Yc

Support, celebrate, and grow your best teachers so that they stay in your school and continue to have maximum impact. Burnout and teacher turnover are on the rise, yet we often spend more of our energy on the underperformers. In this powerful book from bestselling authors Todd Whitaker, Connie Hamilton, Joseph Jones, and T.J. Vari, you'll learn why it's crucial to recognize your best teachers, going beyond superficial gestures of appreciation and investing in them in deeper ways.

The authors show school leaders how to identify their best teachers and then reveal strategies for supporting them, including recognizing the value-cost of teachers' time; prioritizing appreciation; controlling the narrative; tailoring professional learning; helping teachers grow through peer observations as well as beyond the school; applying data informed feedback; and nurturing self- and collective-efficacy. Each chapter begins with a powerful story, an overview of our blind spots, strategies on what we should invest in, and how to ensure that the whole school profits from your efforts. There's also an Initial Deposits feature that provides a quick, tangible way to get started with each idea.

With the helpful models, tips, and tricks in this book, you won't just be inspired to make a change but will be well equipped to take action. As your best teachers get better and better, your students and the entire school culture will benefit!

Todd Whitaker (@toddwhitaker) is a leading presenter in the field of education and has written more than 60 books including the bestseller *What Great Teachers Do Differently*. He is a former teacher, coach, principal, and professor of educational leadership.

Connie Hamilton is a highly sought-after consultant who collaborates with educators to improve teaching and learning. She has served as a teacher, instructional coach, principal, and district curriculum leader. She has authored several books, including *Hacking Questions: 11 Answers that Create a Culture of Inquiry in Your Classroom*.

Joseph Jones is the Superintendent of Schools in the New Castle County Vocational-Technical School District in Delaware. He is a co-founder of TheSchoolHouse302, a leadership development institute, and co-author of *Candid and Compassionate Feedback: Transforming Everyday Practice in Schools.*

T.J. Vari is the Deputy Superintendent of the Appoquinimink School District in Delaware. He is a co-founder of TheSchoolHouse302, a leadership development institute, and co-author of *Candid and Compassionate Feedback: Transforming Everyday Practice in Schools.*

Also Available from Routledge Eye on Education
(www.routledge.com/k-12)

What Great Teachers Do Differently, 3rd Edition: Nineteen Things That Matter Most
Todd Whitaker

What Great Principals Do Differently, 3rd Edition: Twenty Things That Matter Most
Todd Whitaker

Leading School Change, 2nd Edition: How to Overcome Resistance, Increase Buy-in, and Accomplish Your Goals
Todd Whitaker

Your First Year: How to Survive and Thrive as a New Teacher
Todd Whitaker, Katherine Whitaker, and Madeline Whitaker Good

Classroom Management from the Ground Up
Todd Whitaker, Katherine Whitaker, and Madeline Whitaker Good

Dealing with Difficult Parents, 2nd Edition
Todd Whitaker and Douglas Fiore

Dealing with Difficult Teachers
Todd Whitaker

A School Leader's Guide to Dealing with Difficult Parents
Todd Whitaker and Douglas Fiore

Invest in Your Best

9 Strategies to Grow, Support, and Celebrate Your Most Valuable Teachers

Todd Whitaker, Connie Hamilton,
Joseph Jones, and T.J. Vari

Routledge
Taylor & Francis Group

NEW YORK AND LONDON

First published 2024
by Routledge
605 Third Avenue, New York, NY 10158

and by Routledge
4 Park Square, Milton Park, Abingdon, Oxon, OX14 4RN

Routledge is an imprint of the Taylor & Francis Group, an informa business

Library of Congress Cataloging-in-Publication Data
Names: Whitaker, Todd, 1959- author. | Hamilton, Connie, author. | Jones,
Joseph (Educator), author. | Vari, T. (T. J.) author.
Title: Invest in your best : 9 strategies to grow, support, and celebrate
your most valuable teachers / Todd Whitaker, Connie Hamilton, Joseph
Jones, T.J. Vari.
Description: New York, NY : Routledge, 2024. | Series: Routledge eye on
education | Includes bibliographical references.
Identifiers: LCCN 2023032122 | ISBN 9781032342788 (hardback) | ISBN
9781032331386 (paperback) | ISBN 9781003321316 (ebook)
Subjects: LCSH: Teacher morale. | Teacher turnover. | Teachers--Job
satisfaction. | Teacher-administrator relationships.
Classification: LCC LB2840 .W44 2024 | DDC 371.1001/9--dc23/eng/20231019
LC record available at https://lccn.loc.gov/2023032122

ISBN: 978-1-032-34278-8 (hbk)
ISBN: 978-1-032-33138-6 (pbk)
ISBN: 978-1-003-32131-6 (ebk)

DOI: 10.4324/9781003321316

Typeset in Palatino
by SPi Technologies India Pvt Ltd (Straive)

Access the Support Material: www.routledge.com/9781032331386

Contents

Meet the Authors

Dr. Todd Whitaker has been fortunate to be able to blend his passion with his career. Recognized as a leading presenter in the field of education, his message about the importance of teaching has resonated with hundreds of thousands of educators around the world. Todd is a professor of educational leadership at the University of Missouri, and he has spent his life pursuing his love of education by researching and studying effective teachers and principals.

Prior to moving into higher education he was a mathematics teacher and basketball coach in Missouri. Todd then served as a principal at the middle school, junior high, and high school levels. He was also a middle school coordinator in charge of staffing, curriculum, and technology for the opening of new middle schools.

One of the nation's leading authorities on staff motivation, teacher leadership, and principal effectiveness, Todd has written over 60 books including the national bestseller, *What Great Teachers Do Differently*. Other titles include: *Shifting the Monkey, Dealing with Difficult Teachers, The 10 Minute Inservice, The Ball, What Great Principals Do Differently, Motivating & Inspiring Teachers,* and *Dealing with Difficult Parents*.

Todd is married to Beth, also a former teacher and principal, who is the coordinator of the Educational Leadership program at the University of Missouri. They are the parents of three children: Katherine, Madeline, and Harrison.

Connie Hamilton, Ed.S. is committed to supporting teachers and school leaders everywhere. She spends the majority of her time working side by side with teachers and leaders in schools and classrooms across the United States. She is a highly sought-after consultant and speaker who collaborates with educators to improve teaching and learning.

In over two decades of service to the field of education, Connie has served as a teacher, instructional coach, principal at both the elementary and secondary levels, and district curriculum leader. She has authored several books for teachers and school leaders including *Hacking Group Work: 11 Ways to Build Student Engagement, Accountability, and Cooperation With Collaborative Teams, Hacking Questions: 11 Answers that Create a Culture of Inquiry in Your Classroom, Amplify Learner Voice through Culturally Responsive and Sustaining Assessment,* and *Strained and Drained: Tools for Overworked Teachers.*

Often referred to as the "Questioning Guru," Connie is known for her interactive workshops where the best practice methods are modeled to make a learning experience for adults that is active and effective. She has the perfect blend of research and application. Her strategies and methods are based on best practices, but are practical enough that they can be implemented tomorrow to amplify student learning. She strives to support all educators in this challenging but critical role we play for the students who are our future.

Connie is the mother of three adult children. Trey is an artist and designer, Luke serves in the United States Marine Corps, and Allie is working toward a degree in social work.

Joseph Jones, Ed.D., is the Superintendent of the New Castle County Vocational-Technical School District in Delaware. Joe is a former high school social studies teacher, assistant principal, and principal. As principal of Delcastle Technical High School, he was named the Delaware Secondary Principal of the Year, and during his tenure Delcastle was the first high school in Delaware to receive the state's Outstanding Academic Achievement Award. He earned his doctorate from  the University of Delaware in educational leadership and was awarded the outstanding doctoral student award of his class. In his current role as Superintendent, he focuses on ensuring that NCCVT delivers world-class career and technical programs combined with rigorous academics. Additionally, he works closely with local and state leaders on student achievement, spearheading an aggressive campaign to ensure students are successful in high school and in their post-secondary pursuits.

Joe presents nationally on topics of school leadership and is the co-founder of the leadership development institute, TheSchoolHouse302. Along with T.J. Vari, he co-authored *Candid and Compassionate Feedback: Transforming Everyday Practice in Schools*. With Salome Thomas-EL and T.J. Vari, he co-authored three books on school leadership: *Passionate Leadership: Creating a Culture of Success in Every School, Building a Winning Team: The Power of a Magnetic Reputation and the Need to Recruit Top Talent in Every School*, and *Retention for a Change: Motivate, Inspire, and Energize Your School Culture*. He also co-authored *7 Mindshifts for School Leaders: Finding New Ways to Think About Old Problems* with Connie Hamilton and T.J. Vari.

Joe and his wife, an elementary special education teacher, are the proud parents of three sons.

Dr. T.J. Vari is the Assistant Super-intendent of Secondary Schools and District Operations in the Appoquinimink School District in Delaware. He is a former middle school assistant principal and principal and former high school English teacher and department chair. His master's degree is in School Leadership and his doctorate is in Innovation and Leadership where he accepted an Award for Academic Excellence given to one doctoral student per graduating class.

He holds several honors and distinctions, including his past appointment as President of the Delaware Association for School Administrators, his work with the Delaware Association for School Principals, and the honor in accepting the Paul Carlson Administrator of the Year Award.

His efforts span beyond the K-12 arena into higher education where he holds adjunct appointments, teaching courses at the masters and doctoral level. He is a national presenter on topics of school leadership and the co-founder of TheSchoolHouse302, a leadership development institute.

T.J. is a co-author of six educational leadership books, including *Candid and Compassionate Feedback: Transforming Everyday Practice in Schools*; *Passionate Leadership: Creating a Culture of Success in Every School*; *Building a Winning Team: The Power of a Magnetic Reputation and the Need to Recruit Top Talent in Every School*; *Retention for a Change: Motivate, Inspire, and Energize Your School Culture*; and *7 Mindshifts for School Leaders: Finding New Ways to Think About Old Problems*.

T.J. and his wife, Andreina, are the proud parents of Madison and Noah.

Support Material

Several of the handouts from this book are also available on our website as free downloads so you can print them for your own use. They are indicated by this logo ●. To access the downloadable versions, you can go to the book's product page at www.routledge.com/9781032331386 and click on the link that says Support Material.

Introduction

The intersection of ideas and beliefs among a group of people can be powerful. This project was incredibly exciting for us because we were all grappling with how to support school leaders so that they can make greater investments in their best teachers to lift the whole system. Each of us has worked with truly exceptional educators, and we realize that they provide our schools and our students with invaluable gifts. We also know that they put tremendous pressure and expectations on themselves to do so. And as leaders, one of our responsibilities is to attract great people, retain the best of them, and celebrate the impact that our super star educators have on everyone with whom they interact. The other reason that we focus on the best is because they exhibit the qualities of a teacher that all students deserve.

Let's face it, the best teachers have a school-wide (at a minimum) vision and a desire to assist everyone to be successful. This includes the school leaders. Outstanding educators are highly aware that for them to maximize their impact on students, their leaders have to have a positive impact on everyone in the organization too. Because of this, it is imperative that leaders effectively recruit, cultivate, and support the very best educators so that they can help us as leaders to become our best. It's this cycle of growth that matters most. We help our most valuable teachers and, in turn, they help us and everyone else.

One problem is that high achieving educators are often so focused on others that they may lose sight of making sure that they are taken care of as well. That is at the core of this book. We must consistently and continually support, appreciate, and grow them as they spend so much of their energy on the greater good. If a school loses one of their best teachers, everyone in the setting suffers. We're talking about the kind of educators who break new ground, plant the seeds, and help cultivate growth and change. Without them, schools are stagnant, no matter how much the leader wants to bring about change. Every great school leader knows who their best teachers are and understands that everyone else in the school rises and falls based on how we view the best of us. The truth is that when we take care of our teachers it allows them to take care of their students. The same goes with our best people; when we take good care of them, it spreads among the others to profit the whole school, including the students. And, if leaders fail to do so they might lose the most valuable asset in their schools.

Effective leaders know that positive student outcomes are always linked back to the classroom teacher. In the age where the primary responsibility of the principal is to be an instructional leader, much of their attention is placed on ensuring that every classroom teacher is effective. We applaud leaders who are intent on building a school that will support quality teaching practices and better student outcomes. However, it's common for leaders to focus on what may *not* be working and end up spending their time on the lowest performing third of their staff. This approach particularly impacts their plan for communication, professional development, and the observation and feedback cycle.

The problem with this is that it perpetuates a deficit-based mindset, placing a focus on weaknesses and not strengths. In the end, leaders may pay a price for placing more attention on the lower performing teachers because it means that they could end up overlooking the development, care, and appreciation of their best teachers. Yet, if leaders embrace an asset-based mindset, directed to investing in our greatest teachers, they will not only be lifted and empowered, they will positively impact the whole school.

That's the bottom line of this book – to shift school leaders' mindsets from deficit-based thinking to asset-based thinking. We want school leaders to embrace that school transformation, student success, and school improvement are far more likely to occur when we invest in our best teachers. Before we say more about what you'll encounter in the book, let's explore why this happens in schools – why do school leaders end up feeling compelled to work with their lowest performers, overlooking the best?

Be on the lookout for common mindset traps that instructional leaders might fall into if they make any of these three assumptions about their most valuable teachers:

1. **The Growth of the Best Teachers Is Inevitable**. School leaders know (or assume) that the best teachers will make gains regardless of the time that we invest in them. While this may work to some degree, they also have the most potential to make improvements based on intentional growth-oriented activities. Sure, they'll grow on their own, but you'll see what happens if you make investments in them beyond what happens naturally for our best teachers. Also, be aware that the very best people want to improve. If you do not assist them in this growth they may look for another leader elsewhere who can partner with them in their improvement.

2. **The Talents of the Best Teachers Are Used for Others**. Instead of directly investing in the best teachers, school leaders use them to invest in other staff members, either the lower performing of teachers or through general professional development at faculty meetings. This also seems like a logical move but it often ends up creating more work for the people who are likely already working the hardest. We can find ways for this to occur that are also investments in the best people versus a punishment for being exceptional.

3. **The Expertise of the Best Teachers Creates Conflict**. Many school leaders simply don't know *how* to invest in their best. It may be because of their own limitations within the content area that the teacher teaches, it could be because they're not sure that they have much to offer in the way of support for growth, and most often it's because we are intimidated by the best people based on the (potentially correct) conclusion that they are more talented than we are. We'll help you get past that so that you can invest in teachers even if they are so amazing that you're unsure of how to help. Leaders should remember when anyone in their organization looks good, some of that light always shines on the leader.

These traps create mediocrity. The greatest players on the team aren't receiving the attention they deserve to get better and the lower third aren't improving enough to benefit the whole school (perhaps, not any part of it). It's important to share that often-times these missteps are unintentional. The job of a school leader is vast and ever-expanding, built on the pressure to succeed and improve student outcomes. Of course, the natural inclination for any leader is to target the things and people that appear to be "broken" and "fix" them.

That said, we hope that this book points out that our super-stars are so valuable in terms of our investment in them that they should be the *first* place that we look to spend our time and energy. By developing and growing your most valuable teach-ers, you're making an investment in the overall stock of your school. When your best teachers get better, they have the power to transform the whole place – culture, growth, achievement, and morale. We must also be aware that the best employees have a greater chance to leave than anyone else in our school. Why? Because they are more talented and can apply their talents to anything and any profession. And, if one of them departs, they'll likely leave a hole that can never be refilled.

What we hope for readers is that you'll uncover ways to grow, support, and celebrate your most valuable teachers so that they stay in your school and have the maximum impact that they can have on everyone else. We provide models, tips, tricks, sug-gestions, and more. Let's get started with how we think about and define our best teachers and their position among everyone else in our efforts to improve school outcomes.

The Best Teachers

Before we go any further, it's important to know who we are referring to when we say, "best teachers." We're not keen on labels and categories, but there's a reality to the performance of any staff in any profession. Ask any random administrator who their best teachers are, and they can rattle them off in a jiffy, and we assume that you have probably already started that thinking process yourself given that you're reading this book. Before we

move forward into the heart of the strategies we're going to provide you, let's look at a definition for what it means to be among
the best teachers in a school.

One way of thinking about any group of employees, and in
this case with the focus on educators, comes from the book *What
Great Principals Do Differently* (2020). In it, Al Burr is cited as sharing that there are three types of teachers: superstars, backbones,
and mediocres. Our best teachers typically fall into the superstar
category. Here are four quick guidelines as we think of teachers
who are superstars:

1. Former students remember them as their best teachers.
2. Parents regularly request these teachers for their children –
   or wish their children had them as their teacher.
3. Their peers respect these teachers.
4. If they left your school, you probably would not be able
   to hire replacements of the same caliber.

Of these qualities, the one that requires the leader to handle with
the most care is the third – that they are respected by their peers.
It is a rare person that is better than most of their colleagues but
does so with the vulnerability to garner respect. Too often, when
we encounter people with larger-than-life skills, they also exhibit
arrogance. It is challenging for many teachers to just fit in with
peers, let alone deal with the truth that their pedagogical skills
exceed others – and they know it. Simply put, it is very difficult
to balance the dichotomy of being better than others and fitting
in with them simultaneously. This is where superstars differ –
they bring all four of these characteristics to your school, and
instead of posing a threat to others, they make the people around
them better too.

Another way to think about our best teachers is that in
addition to our all around just generally best teachers, we also
have others who haven't necessarily reached their pinnacle but
who are still some of our best teachers in one or more specific
areas that support students and the school. And, sometimes we
don't even know who they are. They may be new and not well
known in the school yet. They may be shy to the point that their

colleagues do not understand the gifts that they bring to their classroom. They may be dynamic with students but more of an introvert with adults. These good people have rare gifts but are not quite as well rounded or as popular as superstars. However, they may also be difficult to replace, which is important to remember.

We will share more about what defines a "best teacher" in the feature below but wanted to preface it by helping you understand the delicate dance that becomes the responsibility of the leader when treating them differently while not hurting their connectivity with colleagues. No matter how good they are with students, if they are not respected by their peers, they lose the ability to influence others as significantly as we would like them to. And, the strategies in this book work best when the superstars are respected and viewed with admiration. Additionally, the superstars are almost always the principal's pet but they can never be *perceived as being* the principal's pet. Great school leaders learn to elevate the status of the best teachers so that their superpowers rub off on everyone else without alienating them as "favorites." Let's take a look at a broader definition of *the best* with this framework of what we've described about their treatment.

"THE BEST"

The first thing you ought to know is that your most valuable teachers are superstars. They may not want or expect that label, but they are. Typically, they are an externally humble group, which means that regardless of whether or not they are actually humble, they work to act like it so that they do not lose the respect of their peers. Some of them – while making huge contributions to the school's success – can fly under the radar as they do it. Yet others are very charismatic and outgoing. "The Best" can fall into either category.

But don't get us wrong, we're not saying to go around labeling or publicly calling your superstars out as the "best." That wouldn't be fair to them or anyone else and would likely negatively impact your school culture. What we're saying is that you need to know who they are and appreciate the gifts that they have as well as the gifts that they bring to your school. And, many of them might need more of a differentiated approach to growth and support than your other teachers – the backbones and the mediocres (more on this after we clearly define "the best").

Teaching is unlike many other professions in how nuanced and complex it can be, but it's not unlike other professions in the variance of skill and ability that dozens or even hundreds of individuals bring to their workplace. Some teachers are simply more skilled and perform better in the classroom than the rest of the pack. Until we recognize and appreciate that, we'll continue to fall short of what they need.

We also want to acknowledge a potential trap, which is guilt. Knowing who your best teachers are and feeling guilty about naming them in your mind is an important point to take with you as you continue to read. The definition of leadership is influence. The challenge of leadership is conflict. The result of leadership is change. In this case, the conflict is the guilt that you have in accepting that some teachers are just better than others. If we feel obligated to treat everyone the same, it is truly a disservice to each person and often more so to the most talented.

We all have that guilt because it stems from not wanting to label teachers and not wanting to admit that there are differences in the student experience, based on who you assign to them for instruction. The result of leadership, with this understanding in mind, is that we change our approach to supporting teachers from across the spectrum of their expertise. One primary call-to-action in this book is a differentiated approach to professional development. Your best teachers need something different than everyone else. You know that about your struggling teachers; we need to accept that it's also true about the best. We're sure that your guilt will subside as you read and learn *how* to differentiate support for teachers.

The first step is that we must clearly identify our best teachers in as much of an objective way as possible. The last thing you want to do is to create any semblance of favoritism through your actions and what you provide for this select group, which will be visible to every other teacher in your school in most cases. You need to be able to defend your choices when pressed for a rationale by any teacher who sees differentiated treatment as something that they're *not* getting. With that said, we have four primary factors that we use to determine "the best." We also know that every school leader has their own definition in mind. That is okay too, yet the approaches that we take to supporting and retaining them remain the same. One final note, one or more of these characteristics can apply to people who are not superstars but who are definitely in the high backbone category. This is important to know because it will help you as you read and think about applying the different strategies in this book to both your superstars and your potential superstars.

1. Your best teachers often stand out to everyone as the ***most positive*** people on staff. They are always up for a challenge, and they see everything through a positive lens and an optimistic outlook. If someone ever challenged you with, "Why does Cindi get to go to The Power of Positive Leadership Certified Training Program with Jon Gordon?" you need to be able to say, "Cindi is one of the most positive people on staff, we need her to learn even more about how to develop positive leaders in our school." In saying that aloud, the person asking should simply agree. We also know that *should agree* does not mean that they *will agree*. If we are concerned with the perception of Cindi going alone to the training as favoritism of some sort, we have options. One option is that rather than just sending Cindi alone, we could send her with a couple of other really solid teachers (backbones) so that she is not isolated. The benefit of this option is that not only is Cindi getting the training, she's also able to help move the others forward in an acceptable manner to all. This way, we prevent Cindi from being looked at as a kiss-up in the school. We'll say more about this type of thing throughout the book.

2. Your best teachers are the *strongest contributors* to new, quality initiatives and programs at your school that will have a positive impact on students and families. They are seen as powerhouses beyond their classroom. They lead the new reading initiative – either as a formal leader or just as often by being the informal leader. They run the data PLCs. They plan the new Restorative Practices workshops. They're on the Grading Committee. When you need something to get lifted from the ground-up and then to permeate the rest of the staff, you think of these people first. And whatever role they play – formal or informal – they seem to always arrive with a smile, ready to get their hands dirty. Again, as a leader, we want to balance how their influence can be most impactful while helping them to maintain the respect that they deserve from their peers.

3. Your best teachers have a *growth mindset*. They are never content with the status quo of their work. Constantly reflecting and revising, they push themselves to take risks and improve practice. They're already hungry; they just need a unique approach to satisfy their desire to get better. It's why they are perfect for the strategies in this book. They compare themselves to perfection, which pushes them forward but becomes a point of sensitivity for leaders who want to help them grow. We don't want to just let them beat themselves up over things that didn't go perfectly, but we want them to take risks with things that might not go well the first time. The strategies in this book help to foster their growth mindset and give them a platform for seeing progress as a better predictor of success than perfection.

4. Lastly, they also *get results*. They consistently demonstrate the greatest student growth based on a variety of measures. Performance, proficiency, skill acquisition, talent refinement, and other assessment results all validate that when students spend time with these teachers they improve academically, artistically, athletically, musically, socially, and more. These teachers look at the whole child

within and beyond their content area. Your best teacher may be a PE teacher, a first-grade teacher, or your band director. They clearly have the strongest abilities. Their instincts are often in line with research, whether they can cite it or not, and they use evidence-based practices with precision.

But, beyond the visible aspects of their teaching, this top group of teachers consistently demonstrate that they are valuable. They build quality relationships with students which often result in fewer discipline referrals. Individual learners who might have made less effort in the past develop a level of motivation to engage and learn from these teachers. Their names surface again-and-again in school surveys when students reference teachers who inspired, influenced, or otherwise made a lasting impact on them. Year-after-year, students learn and improve in their classrooms. Whatever the goals may be – behavioral, career-and-technical certification, academic, social – it doesn't matter. Your best teachers meet the goals, objectively, on paper.

One more thing that we want to say about defining your "best teachers" is that you can use other criteria, in addition to our four or instead of the ones we've listed. You might rank your teachers in terms of the number of parent requests you get each year. You might create a complex tracking system using a whole host of indicators, such as student time on task, quality of questions, or similar instructional methods you notice in walk-throughs. Your top teachers will have more frequency in the times these actions are observed. What matters is that you're as objective as possible and that you can articulate your rationale for identifying them as the superstars. Why? Because people may ask why you're investing in them differently than others. And, the less you isolate them, the less you need to rationalize differentiating them from others.

Even though you won't go putting signs above their doors with BEST TEACHER flashing lights, people will notice the opportunities given to this elite group. That's all part of a culture where the top performers get the respect that they earn and deserve from you, their peers, families, and the community. And although we trust your spidey-supervisory-senses, your intuition has biases that could cloud your judgment more than you realize. Using an objective approach doesn't just protect you from scrutiny, it shields you and your best teachers from your own misconceptions about teachers.

Lastly, this is no time to be afraid. When you identify and lift your best teachers, the whole system profits. We'll show you how to give your best teachers a boost at the same time improving the culture for everyone else so that people are much less likely to question what you're doing.

Defining the Best

Now that you know how to define your best teachers, we want to bring up two other groups of teachers that we'll reference as we unfold our investment strategies throughout the book. The first group we refer to as *backbones* and the second we call the *mediocres*. This concept was described in *Dealing with Difficult Teachers* (Whitaker, 2015) and attributed to Dr. Al Burr. The basic premise is that you have three categories of teachers in every school: *superstars*, *backbones*, and *mediocres*.

We've already defined *superstars* for you; they're your best teachers. Burr explains this group as only being about 3–10% of the total population of teachers. The *backbones* are the majority, maybe 80–90% of your teachers. The best thing you can do for backbones is to help them to perform like superstars. The backbones are just as they're described. They are the working backbone of the school. Most teachers fall into this category, and although you want them on your side in terms of school improvement, you can afford to lose a few of them while others are very much irreplaceable – similar to the superstars.

The backbones often possess skills and talents that would position them at being the best at something. For example, they might be the best with embedding technology into their lessons that meaningfully engages students. Perhaps, they're the best at connecting with students on a personal level. Or they might even be the best at a particular strategy, such as managing centers and small group instruction. It's important to keep these strengths in mind as you're looking to elevate your entire staff. While your superstars find success in nearly all facets of teaching, the backbones have a key role in elevating the whole system too.

That brings us to the third category, *mediocres*. "Generally mediocre teachers are ineffective in the classroom. Additionally, they can provide other challenges that compound the burden they place on a school and its leader" (Whitaker, 2015). Mediocres are almost always difficult to deal with, and although some backbones can be difficult as well, mediocres provide limited value and generally you can find someone who is more beneficial to your school and more importantly, to your students. You'll learn more about these categories as you read, but we wanted to set the context up front about how you should define superstar (best teachers) and everyone else as you begin to differentiate your approach to school leadership.

Also, please keep in mind that one responsibility is to hire superstars and another one is to cultivate them. This is not a stagnant label. It is much more a formative test than a summative one. That is what great leaders work to do. They also work to identify components of teachers that make them irreplaceable, to highlight and accentuate them, to build confidence, and to support the quality of the school. Additionally, the best leaders help mediocres move to backbones and backbones move to superstars. We're always leveling up, which is exactly what our strategies in this book will help you do with your top teachers.

So many teachers have some of the gifts and components necessary to be great but not all of the components at the same time. If you have a talented teacher who works well with students but who struggles with peer relations, we can work on that. They're on their way to superstardom, and you can help them by working with them in the areas where they need to grow. You may even have teachers who are excellent at one or a few things that can be showcased as they move along the continuum in other areas. Highlighting where they have talents will help them build their other skills. You have your all around best, but you also have a few backbones who are "the best" in a single area. We can use that for the betterment of everyone else just like we're going to lift the whole system by investing in our best teachers. Remember, we are in the improvement business, not the perfection business. Let's talk about the structure of the book so that you can get the most out of it.

The Structure of the Book

Your reading experience will be more effective and efficient if you're aware of what you'll encounter as you read. Every chapter is set up the same way – for both ease of use and flow. Each chapter is focused on a different strategy as an investment in your best teachers. We hope that you're inspired by what you read, but this book is not written for inspiration; it's written for action. We hope that you'll find enjoyment in the stories that we share to begin each chapter, and we hope that you'll see why our blind spots, identified as "costs," are such problems for continuous improvements in schools. In each chapter, we tell you exactly what great teachers need with examples, strategies, and models that work for getting them greater levels of support. And, in each, we provide a tip for maximizing your investment so that the whole school profits from your efforts. Here's the breakdown that each chapter follows:

Simple Story
Each chapter starts with a simple story that demonstrates the impact of an investment in your best teachers. The stories are real although some of the names have been changed. Some stories are from experiences in our own schools, others are from the partnerships we have as consultants, and a few are from the business world that we gathered as we wrote the book. We hope that you'll see how the various stories set the stage for each investment strategy.

The Cost of Not Investing
This section, we keenly named as the "cost" because flawed thinking in schools can hold us back from our most successful work. We can't continue to expect new and different results by doing the things that we've always done to get them. You may even see yourself, your school, or a former leader in some of the costly

decision-making that we outline, and that's okay. Just know that we're moving on to a new strategy.

Your Investment Strategy

This section provides you with a new model for investing in your best teacher. Get ready for our acronyms. Most of the models include acronyms so that you can easily remember and expertly implement the strategy. We provide steps, sections, tips, and resources as we unfold the ways in which you can make investments in your best teachers that will also be investments in the whole school.

Maximizing Your Investment

In our "maximizing" sections, you'll get a pro-level tip for how to think about or execute the investment to make sure that it works to the best of its ability. If you could get a few more percentage points higher on your financial investments, you would, and these sections show you how to up the percentage in the return on the strategy you're using to lift your best teachers.

Profiting the Whole System

As we finish each chapter, we're explicit with how the strategy you're using with your best teachers will either work the same way or have benefits for everyone else. In some cases, you may just want to tweak the strategy for every teacher; in other cases, you'll see how everyone earns dividends when our best teachers soar.

The Bottom Line

The Bottom Line is the conclusion and final thoughts about each chapter. It's not a summary, but it does drive home some of the key points we want you to take away as a leader. Plus, there's always a bottom line, and, as leaders, we need to know it.

Initial Deposits

The Initial Deposits sections are a feature at the end of each chapter that help you to think about the first steps as well as how you might use the strategy in a way that works for you.

Every school and every school leader is starting from a different point, and your context matters. You can use these strategies whether you're a small rural school with only a few teachers or a large urban school with a huge staff. This feature will help you to get going. You won't finish any of the chapters or learn about any of the strategies and think: "Where do I begin?" We have you covered.

Let's get started!

1

Making a Blue Ocean Shift

Toilet Paper, Value-Cost, and Teachers' Time

If you were going to open a business, would you want to sell something that everyone else offers or would you want to be the only one with a particular product? That's the difference between a blue ocean strategy and entering into a red ocean scenario. A blue ocean strategy is found when the market opens up without much struggle to generate business and profits from a new or different product. The blue ocean is wide open without the fierce competition of other similar goods or services. In a red ocean, it's all blood and carnage; everyone is thrashing around for space in the market. Authors of *Blue Ocean Shift* (Mauborgne & Kim, 2017) describe this concept in detail in their case study regarding Kimberly-Clark Brazil's (KCB) blue ocean shift in a $1.5 billion dollar toilet tissue industry where the way that toilet paper was manufactured was highly competitive, creating a red ocean. No one was thinking about producing and distributing toilet paper any differently than their competitors.

That's when KCB decided to take a hard look at their product innovations and held what the authors call a "blue ocean fair." Essentially, KCB engineers pitched new ways that consumers could view and find value in the KCB toilet paper line. After evaluating several ideas, one blue ocean shift emerged as the winner.

DOI: 10.4324/9781003321316-1

A compressed size toilet paper roll, called *Just One Hug*, allowed customers to buy a smaller size toilet paper roll that included the same amount of paper as the larger rolls.

In the Brazilian market, this was a significant innovation due to transportation issues. People carrying large packages home from the grocery store by means of public transit isn't easy. The new toilet paper line, *Just One Hug*, allowed users to carry much smaller packages with easier mobility and greater storage capacity. You can imagine traveling with a 12 toilet paper package on the bus and then trying to store it in a small apartment. KCB changed all of that with a new packaging innovation that created a blue ocean, wide open market in an otherwise red ocean, highly competitive economy for toilet paper. Not only was this an incredible new benefit for the Brazilian consumers, it was also revolutionary for KCB. With a 15% reduction in transportation costs, 19% decrease in packaging materials, and a gross margin greater than 20%, it was a winner for the toilet paper industry and KCB as a leader.

By looking at what they were doing differently it allowed them to have a fresh approach. Before the car was first invented, if we asked people what they wanted, they would have said, "a faster horse." There are people in your school who already want to find new and better approaches. We just have to find them, support them, and entrust them. These visionaries have more confidence to make a dramatic leap, which can lead us to an area with less competition.

So, you may be wondering why this matters for teachers? One, school leaders should think more about the value-cost of teachers' time and ask, how do we really want our teachers spending their time? What maximizes their efforts toward teaching and learning? Two, as we think about our best teachers, how can we employ a blue ocean shift to their time? In other words, we need to ensure that our teachers' time, particularly our best teachers, is spent in the best ways. That requires us to think about applying new strategies to their experiences in our schools that are different from what we do for every other teacher. Your best teachers need a blue ocean shift, and school leaders can invest in that shift by using our T.I.M.E. Model.

The Costs Associated With Ignoring Time Factors

One of our theories about the challenges associated with recruiting and retaining educators is that we have one of the most rigid working schedules of any profession. Teachers can't be late, they can't use the bathroom at their own leisure, they can't attend appointments without taking time off, and they always have to be ready for the show. The show, we call it, of being an actor of sorts in front of our students, period-after-period, day-after-day.

Although the schedule is rigid and poses limitations, teaching itself is a blessing. We put on a show to impress upon our students the facts, challenges, and rewards of our world, including studies in literature, art, mathematics, world history, and a host of other subjects to engage them as learners. But, any teacher or school leader who is reading this knows that it's exhausting. The grueling nature of a day in the life of a teacher demonstrates that the people in this profession are resilient, creative, persistent, and, above all, selfless. Our superstars are those things on their worst day. On their best days, they're practically superheroes.

But their ability to master their day doesn't diminish the problem that most educators don't have enough time in their day or week to accomplish everything required of them. Education continues to grow in complexity as it is recognized as the central hub of our communities. Whether it be ongoing curriculum expansion within a limited time, or the need to offer additional social and emotional advisory periods, teachers are constantly asked to do more without additional time. The problem is that everything is viewed equally in value so nothing is cut back. Teachers aren't saying "no" to very many responsibilities because most of what they get tasked with doing fulfills a need for students.

That said, what teachers don't get, and the very best teachers are among them, is any consideration for differentiation of time and activities. Still, as we write this book, a single teacher's time is treated the same as every other teachers' time. If one person has a duty, everyone has one. Even worse is that sometimes the average teacher has three committees and the best people have ten.

That can be more of a time drain and is essential to balance and actually takes pressure off of someone being seen as the favorite or the goody two shoes.

As we will call out in Chapter 4, if a professional development series is offered to one group of teachers, often it's the same for everyone. Time in schools is allocated equally across all of our teachers, and, yet, teachers use time differently depending on what we call *The Three Es of Teacher Time: Experiences, Effectiveness, and Endurance.* When leaders make decisions about teachers' time, and in this case our best teachers' time, we have to consider all three Es. Let's dig deeper.

You must start thinking about your best teachers' time differently than you do about everyone else on staff. As a side note, it's possible that you may not currently be asking the most ineffective people to do much at all. That causes resentment with the rest of the staff. It's time to reflect on how much you ask of your superstars versus your backbones versus your mediocres. If the workload isn't distributed properly, which doesn't necessarily mean that it's "even," you could have a problem.

Next time you're about to put something on the calendar or require teachers to complete a training, think from the lens of your best teachers. Teachers' past *experiences* should dictate their reality in schools when it comes to the time constraints that we place on them. Note that we use experiences in the plural form. We're not just referring to years of experience, which matters as well but not nearly as much as the talents they possess and bring with them to the job, regardless of how many years they've had to pack those experiences into. Your best teachers don't need what your new teachers need, they don't need what your backbone teachers need, and they certainly don't need what your mediocre teachers need. Conversely, the mediocre teachers' needs may be different than other staff members also.

The second E focuses on teacher *effectiveness* This also has to be considered when we implement time consuming programs, procedures, and practices. If Mrs. James is awesome at using Kagan strategies, why would we include her in this year's Kagan professional learning series, especially if it's a reset for new teachers and those who need to boost their usage? We're not saying that you should have this teacher run the series either; we're merely reiterating that one-size-fits-all models don't work and that the teacher should have a say in how she learns and grows during professional learning. Then, have the gumption to reply to other teachers who ask why she's not here for the PL in some fashion with a statement like this, "Sandy is already applying these strategies successfully. This introductory workshop doesn't match her needs."

As we point out in other chapters, your best teachers need things, including professional learning, tailored for them more so than your backbones and mediocres. Remember, though, that to be a superstar you have to be respected by your peers. If the best teacher would lose credibility with colleagues by not attending the professional learning or another meeting, it may save them time and cost them grief. One way to balance this is to ask them about it. They want to fit in, and they are well aware of what level of time saved by differentiation is worth the cost of credibility. Sometimes it is, sometimes it isn't. Nothing about investing in your best is a cookie-cutter approach. By the way, your financial adviser will tell you the same about your money. One size almost never fits all.

Finally, teacher *endurance* is a key factor in how much time they have and don't have. Your best teachers are simply powerhouses. They can work harder, faster, and for longer periods of time. It's one of the distinguishing factors in being a superstar teacher. Typically, this means that they take on more responsibilities and produce better results because of their capacity to handle so much. Yet, we fall into the convenience trap of treating them the same as other teachers who aren't at this level of skill and will, combining expertise, drive, and speed.

However, as with all things, our biggest strengths may also be our biggest weaknesses. Our teachers who work harder, faster, and for longer periods obviously have a risk of taking on too much, assuming responsibility for too many things and can multi-task themselves into feeling overwhelmed. Our T.I.M.E. Model helps to avoid this.

School leaders should take note of these assets when allocating time and applying the same pressures to everyone. The best teachers are vulnerable because of their skill set. They can accomplish more in less time and pursue ways to do more for the school, the students, and the community. This is a cautionary tale. School leaders who ignore this warning may end up with exemplary teachers who are burnt-out. Once this happens, the backbones and the mediocres follow quickly thereafter because they often rely on our greatest teachers' efforts to stay afloat. Finding time for superstars and ensuring that all of their time isn't jammed up – even if it's of their own doing – is critical for them to remain at their best and have the degree of influence that we want them to have on the rest of the faculty and students. Let's look at a model that can help you to think about your best teachers' time differently, essentially applying a blue ocean shift to how they use their time to support themselves and the school.

Investment #1: Make Use of T.I.M.E.

It's important that school leaders view and treat their schools as if they were their own small business entrepreneurial endeavor. Successful small business owners typically treat their best employees with love and care, and they don't tolerate poor behaviors because, from a bottom line perspective, they can't. If they did, they would close. As we look at the T.I.M.E. Model, let's remember that it's a shift in the way that we look at our teachers' time, especially the best. The point is to free them up within a "blue ocean" of time rather than having their time lost by competing meetings, initiatives, and unnecessary tasks. Small businesses need their talented staff directed toward the right things to maximize their efforts. They can't afford for anyone's time to be unfocused or lost; that's what we want for our best teachers too.

Target Their Pain Points

The first part of T.I.M.E. is finding out what your best teachers' pain points are in terms of time-wasters. Of course, you can't get rid of all of the minutiae associated with teaching, but our most effective teachers deserve leaders who understand and actively

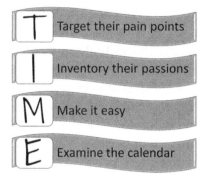

FIGURE 1.1

reduce aspects of the work that are not effective uses of their Three Es – Experiences, Effectiveness, and Endurance.

This is a blue ocean shift for teachers in three powerful ways:

1. It demonstrates how much you care about their time, a commodity that teachers value.
2. It pays off in even better teaching and a greater influence over the school because it will capture time that your best teachers can reinvest in themselves, develop mastery of their craft, or devote to helping others.
3. It demonstrates trust in that you know they have the ability to balance their time with their credibility with peers.

You can set this effort into motion by using an already established meeting time to discuss it. Do yourself a favor and avoid the complete irony of setting up another meeting that they don't want to attend to discuss what's taking all of their time. Instead, use your already identified goal-setting meetings, pre-observation conferences, or another time that feels like a logical time to ask.

Here's what you're asking, "Trent, you're an invaluable part of our team, and I would like to understand more about your major pain points as a teacher here. In other words, what is eating up your time or what are the things that add up to be a waste of your time?" The good news is that your best teachers won't likely name or identify anything that they know is out of anyone's control. Here's another way to ask, "If I could take something off of your plate that would save you time, what would it be?" Now, you just listen intently to what they say.

There are inevitably things that you can't do much about. In that case, we encourage school leaders to discuss them. However, there are things that are in one's span of control, so dig deeper as to why those things are taking up so much time. The challenge here is not to be defensive. Keep an open mind and listen carefully. This is important because you're "mining for gold" – informational gold that may enable you to unlock constraints. Consider how your best teachers are typically rule followers (like most teachers). It's quite possible that they are misinterpreting something that you're asking them to do, making it more complicated and taxing than it needs to be. Superstars are prone to this problem. That's why the first part of asking is about understanding their perspective.

Lastly, do any and everything that you can to get them some amount of time back by reducing the burden that they have and feel. Here's a list of the things that we've seen in the past:

◆ Optional paperwork – like observation, lesson planning, and reflection paperwork – that you might need most teachers to submit but that your best teachers (and you) find unnecessary for this group. Fair and equal are not the same thing, and you might not need to enforce the same set of expectations for task completion consistently across the staff regardless of what you've been told (check your teachers' contract). For example, if you require everyone to turn in lesson plans and you rarely have time to review them anyway, perhaps you could drop this requirement for everyone. While everyone might benefit with having extra time to allocate in other areas, your best teachers have probably been expending more time than others and, therefore, will reap a bigger reward than others.

◆ Duties that are spread out among staff but that you can find some relief for your best teachers to skip. You may need help in common spaces like halls, recess, and lunch, but do we really want to tie up our most productive people by having them push around trash cans?

◆ Scheduled meetings where you're sharing information that your best teachers could actually run. Do we really need them at all of our meetings or can they skip the ones that share information they already have, like the guidelines for administering a State assessment, and find better ways to use their Three Es?

◆ Professional development that's one-size-fits-all. We see this all the time and we tackle this issue head on in Chapter 4. We're training everyone in something that some teachers already know how to do better than the trainer. Let them go and be more productive in a different space.

There are tons of other items that we can scratch off of our best teachers' to-do lists. Embark on a discovery tour of this kind on your own to expose a few things that are taking more time than necessary for everyone. One challenge is that the most talented people are good at so many things that it is tempting to ask them to do a multitude of tasks. Keeping the Three Es in mind – experience, effectiveness, and endurance – can help us remember to only ask them to do the most essential tasks that are absolutely necessary and that only they can do. Additionally, some tasks that seem unimportant are necessary for all teachers, even your best, to do so that they do not get ostracized from everyone else. Bus duty may seem insignificant, but allowing them to skip their one day a month rotation may cause them more harm because of the dissension – and a parallel reduction in influence – which may not be worth the limited trade off of time.

Inventory Their Passions

The next part of T.I.M.E. is to inventory the passions of your superstars in a way that might unleash their talents and keep them energized at work. Research shows that when people are engaged in a passion project, even a hobby or other personal interest, they give more of their discretionary effort in their regular role (Mitchell, 2021). Your best teachers are passionate people, and their passion goes beyond classroom instruction.

Again, please don't schedule a meeting with your best teachers to do this inventory. You'll be able to find other time and space to find out what you need to know by asking two key questions: 1. "Besides being a classroom teacher, which you're incredible at being, what else makes you tick?" and, 2. Once you have them reveal their passion, you ask, "I wonder how that might be incorporated here at school?" Neither of you needs to answer the second question at that time or even in that month or year. The result is that you showed an interest in the person as a human and not just an employee, and one of you might be able to answer the second question one day in a way that supports your best teachers' motivation, inspiration, and energy at work.

Learning what other people's passions are isn't reserved for only your best teachers. Just like the most valuable teachers can be energized by unleashing their talents at work, many others in your school could benefit from the same inspiration and connection to what they love. Some of the things we do to assist our best can also assist the rest.

Make It Easy (When You Can)

The third exercise using the T.I.M.E. Model is one of our favorite activities, and we adapted it from two sources. The first source is an interview that Tim Ferriss conducted with actor Hugh Jackman in which Jackman described that when he's pushing too hard he thinks of what it would be like to just do 85% of whatever he's doing. So often we can get almost, and sometimes more, of the results we want by doing 85% of something rather than all of what it takes to get to 100%. The second source is Gary Keller and Jay Papasan's 2012 book, *The ONE Thing*. Gary has learned and taught others to ask a very simple question that can change our lives: *What's the ONE thing I can do such that by doing it everything else will be easier or unnecessary?* This question helps individuals make progress toward goals (What's the one thing I can do to live healthier?) and set priorities (What's the one thing that is non-negotiable for me to accomplish today?).

We suggest coupling these two strategies with just about everything in schools but especially as it pertains to what we're asking from our best teachers. Of course, you can use this in tandem with the pain point discussion above. You might not be able to take something off of a teacher's plate, but you may have the latitude to cut the time it takes by 15% or solve another seemingly ancillary problem that will save time with the other items.

The key is to understand that we often make the hard parts harder than they need to be and even the easy parts hard. And, your best teachers are the worst culprits; they put 110% into everything, even when it has minimal effect. We have to train our brains to weigh compliance against impact. We can't break too many rules, but we can bend them so that the least impactful time-wasters are accomplished in the easiest ways possible.

Examine the Calendar

The final aspect of the T.I.M.E. Model is to examine the school calendar from the beginning of the school year all the way up into the final days. It's unfortunate, but we find awkward and unproductive uses of teachers' time when we do this analysis. This strategy is one that helps all teachers, but remember that we're specifically thinking through the lens of what our best teachers need.

As we examine the school calendar, we ought to consider the placement of our professional learning days, how many days are allocated for PL to start the school year, how much time we plan to hold teachers on PL days, and even how teachers' planning periods are distributed throughout the day, juxtaposed against other blocks of time. Let's review a few of the most commonly found mistakes that come at a major cost.

First, we find wasted days at the end of school calendars. For a whole host of reasons, calendar committees tolerate unproductive days at the end of the calendar simply because of the number of days that teachers are expected to work (based on state and local policies). It's offensive to make teachers report to work when their work is done for the year, and it's even more offensive to add professional learning to the days before the school year ends. Your best teachers would prefer that these days get front loaded or spread throughout the year for the sake of preparing, learning, creating, reflecting, and growing. If you are not sure what your best teachers want, feel free to ask them. They are very good at looking you in the eye and telling you the truth.

And since they view the school with a very wide lens they often know what others would prefer as well.

Second, we find odd sequences of days that don't make sense for students or teachers. Just recently, we saw a week that was one day on, one day off, two days on, and Friday off. And, it was placed at the end of a grading period. Not only will those days be wasted from a teaching and learning perspective, but they annoy your best teachers who would otherwise use the time for themselves and their students. Your backbones care about this wasted time too, but your mediocre teachers will just let the whole week go by with very little to show for it.

Also, if the professional development isn't of much value overall, not only is that a waste of time to your best, it is a waste of time to everyone else. Worse, it also wastes resources, effort, opportunities, and the list goes on. We hope that thinking about how to invest in your best has some carry-over to how to invest in everyone as many of these concepts apply to everyone who works in the school.

Third, and most egregious, is the amount of "learning" time that is jammed into professional learning days for teachers. Your best teachers will soak in what they learn, and, if given the time, will reflect and produce something. But if time isn't allocated to develop what was learned, then much of the learning is wasted. Organizing and structuring the learning time effectively is crucial. For example, if 7.5 hours constitutes a work day, that doesn't mean that all the time should be used for learning in the form of receiving information. We suggest breaking that up into some time for engaging professional learning, a healthy chunk of time for lunch, and afternoon planning, reflection, and when appropriate, product development time for teachers. Your best teachers will flourish in this structure.

Maximizing Your Investment: Interview Students

If you're not in the habit of interviewing students about their school experiences, this is a great place to start. We recommend interviewing students for a multitude of reasons, including what they'll say about your best teachers. Amplifying student voices not only lifts students but it provides key insights into particular areas of schooling that we may not be seeing. It holds the potential to improve learning and increase students' sense of belonging, and it demonstrates that we care deeply about what they think about and want from school. This effort goes beyond traditional roles that students would possess within clubs or student government and essentially gives them a seat at the table to discuss real issues (Miltra, 2008).

Interviews may seem a little heavy handed or formal; you may discover the same type of information in a less formal setting by asking kids in the lunchroom or at recess. Finding out who their favorite teachers are and why even helps us identify superstars who we might not otherwise peg. Plus, just hearing about these teachers puts you in a positive frame of mind as well.

In terms of your best teachers, students can provide much needed wisdom from anything like how teachers connect with students to how they break down complex information in the classroom. Additionally, we can learn what makes them fun or seem caring. From kindergarten to advanced physics, it is amazing how much the best teachers have in common.

Ultimately, our goal is to get better at supporting our best teachers so that their influence flourishes and so that their skills are replicable for others; this is where student insight is invaluable. With all that has been said about innovation in schools, it might actually just be easier to replicate the bright spots that we already know about. One strategy for knowing more about your bright spots is to ask your students what and who they are. We recommend three primary questions to ask, and we're going to break each one of them down for you in a way that will help you to ask your students about their best teachers. This strategy is meant to maximize the investment that you're already making by using the T.I.M.E. Model.

Question #1: Who Are Our Best Teachers in This School?

Word choice in this first question is critical. We're not looking to get student feedback on who gives more free choice time or who is the easiest grader. We're looking for the individuals who can best help students learn. While there may be overlap between students' *favorite* teachers and the ones who they think are *the best* in the school, they are still very different questions.

When your goal is to identify the best, you may need to keep the students' ages in mind. With elementary students, "favorite" might be a place to start simply because they may have less exposure to multiple teachers. Be sure students are not solely thinking about their homeroom teachers, for example. Sometimes the best teachers are specialists who teach subjects like physical education or art.

Older students are more likely to know the difference between the *best teachers* and their *favorite teachers*, and, depending on who you're asking, these two groups of teachers can be vastly different. Be curious. Using this first question, we're just trying to get a few common names that students mostly agree are "the best." You can use our definition in the front material if you want to help students understand who you're trying to get them to name. This will lead you quickly to question number two.

Question #2: Why Are These Teachers Better Than the Others?

This one will likely need follow-up questions to go with it, like "What makes them the best?" and "How are they different from your other teachers?" You're trying to do two things here. First, you're looking to uncover the strategies, tactics, and practices that the best teachers use so that you can try to replicate them with other staff. Second, you're warming the students up for the last question. We want them to talk all about the things that they believe makes the best teachers the best because in the third question we're going to get them to help us serve the best teachers in ways that we wouldn't have otherwise known to do without the voice of our students.

Question #3: What Do They Need to Keep Being the Best or to Even Get Better?

You'll probably hate to admit it, but there are things that your students know about their teachers' wants and desires that you'll never learn about if you don't ask the kids. Your best teachers are the least likely to complain about the things that are going wrong in their classrooms, and these are things that students see and hear every day. Here's a short list of a few common responses that you might get from this question:

- ◆ Her Smartboard is always acting up. She loses time when it doesn't work right.
- ◆ The announcements are always interrupting his morning meeting. He hates that.
- ◆ The custodians erase important information from the white-board at night, even when she writes "SAVE" on the board.
- ◆ His chair wobbles.
- ◆ They're always bringing in supplies that they bought with their own money.
- ◆ His room is always so cold. He doesn't like when it's cold.

If you want to brace yourself for a fourth question, ask this: "What can I do differently to support our best teachers?" Kids might not always tell the full truth, but with questions like these, you're going to get the FULL TRUTH. That's good news. The final step with this investment is to do something about it that supports your best teachers in ways that you wouldn't have without this critical information from the students. Almost anything you do based on what they say will buy your best teachers more time, comfort, and mental agility to perform in the way that we all know that they can.

How T.I.M.E. Profits the Whole System

It's undeniable that when you target your best teachers' pain points, inventory their passions, make things easier for them, and examine the calendar that they will then get more time and that they'll use that time to do even more great things. That's the obvious part about how the T.I.M.E. Model maximizes your investment in your best teachers so that others benefit too, but there are other profits to be had as well. It's time to consider how these investments also benefit you.

The T.I.M.E. Model is a training mechanism that helps leaders think about teachers' time differently. It challenges the status quo of what we accept in schools as the pressure points and unnecessary burdens for teachers. Too many of our problems in education, even what we would consider to be crises, go unsolved and remain persistent as a result (Hamilton, Jones, & Vari, 2023). When leaders learn to use the T.I.M.E. Model for our best teachers, we learn to look through a different lens for the whole system. It turns our typical red ocean response to all the clutter into a blue ocean that is filled with possibilities.

Not everyone's pain points are the same, neither are their passions or what needs to be made simple. That's also true for how we view the time that we spend with our best teachers as it relates to the yearly, monthly, and weekly calendars we build for the school year. Your best teachers will have some similarities, as will your backbone and mediocre teachers as groups. But, applying the model helps leaders determine the steps that can be made to eliminate the burden on all teachers. The model enables leaders to be better at thinking about the current conditions in schools and what can be done to make them better. That's the blue ocean shift.

Our friend Danny Bauer always says that when the leader gets better we all benefit (Bauer, 2018). That's what our T.I.M.E. Model does for the whole system. When the leader uses T.I.M.E. effectively, we all get more of it. More time means that we can focus on the bigger picture of teaching and learning in school, precisely what our best teachers do best and what we need everyone else to get better at.

 ## The Bottom Line

A blue ocean shift using the T.I.M.E. Model is the kind of mindshift that Connie, Joe, and T.J. wrote about in *7 Mindshifts for School Leaders*. The central argument in that book is that too many of our problems in education are important, urgent, *and* persistent yet don't get treated like the crises that they are (Hamilton, Jones, & Vari, 2023). The bottom line is that when our best teachers' time is consumed with aspects of the job that pull them from what they do best, we have a crisis. We need our best teachers focused and prepared to do their best work.

The one thing that we want to point out as we conclude this chapter is that the T.I.M.E. Model isn't just about time as measured in minutes and hours or days and weeks. A major theme that an effective T.I.M.E. analysis will uncover is about materials, resources, equipment, and other means that support your best teachers so that they're set up to be effective at their jobs. We learned this from *First, Break All the Rules* in terms of the research regarding "what the world's greatest managers do differently" (Gallup, 2016).

Of the 12 items that the Gallup researchers narrowed down to capture the "strengths of a workplace," two of the items were about having the "material and equipment I need to do my work right" and "the opportunity to do what I do best every day" (Gallup, 2016, p. 24). The T.I.M.E. Model helps leaders to significantly impact our best teachers' answers to these two questions. Whether it's you doing the inventory or taking the next step to maximize your investment by interviewing students, your focus on T.I.M.E. will yield great dividends for your superstars.

HOW TO MAKE YOUR INITIAL DEPOSIT

As you think about how you might apply the T.I.M.E. Model, consider taking the smallest step forward that you can easily do in your school tomorrow. We suggest starting with student conversations because you are already around them in the halls, classrooms, and common spaces, and because they're fun to talk to anyway. Use the questions we have in the Maximizing Your Investment section, and don't feel compelled to always ask all three. As you chat with students, using the questions, you'll start to hear themes in their responses. Then, when you have a good gauge on what the students think, you can begin to hash out what it will look like for you to apply the concepts in the T.I.M.E. Model.

2

Prioritizing Appreciation

Where Are the Perks?

Fortune, one of the leading multinational business magazines, provides a list of the 100 best companies to work for. Guess what? There's not a single school on the list.

Anyone seeking to apply to a top 100 company can use filters to narrow down their job search based on perks, benefits, and incentives that employers offer. Some examples include 100% health coverage, unlimited sick days, on-site fitness/subsidized gym memberships, compressed work weeks and remote working options. These are not perks typically offered to public education employees who work in some of the least progressive and most rigid environments we can find.

Looking at benefits like these might cause teachers to think twice about their career choice, even if they love teaching. Who wouldn't be tempted by on-site childcare or college tuition reimbursement? Of course, when you're dealing with tax dollars, the reality is that school budgets have limitations. However, we shouldn't ignore what *can* be done for our teachers.

There are two questions to ask about working conditions that impact teachers. First, what don't teachers get that other professionals do, like Fortune 100 companies such as Cisco and Hilton? And second, how do the decisions within our control communicate and reinforce a lack of appreciation and consideration for our teachers? In fact, much of a teacher's workday is so

DOI: 10.4324/9781003321316-2

restrictive – tied to bells and buses – that it increases their burden, not the other way around.

For example, in tight financial times, school budgets are examined in great detail with the goal of cutting costs. Connie remembers a time when teachers in her school district were forbidden to have personal appliances in their classrooms. No dorm refrigerators (unless there was a medical need), no microwaves, and perhaps the most devastating, no coffee pots. The reasoning was that these appliances required electricity to operate and that money should be used to more directly support student learning.

As the school principal, Connie was tasked to search every classroom for appliances, document what was found, and report the list to the finance office so the teachers could be billed for the estimated electrical expense that the district was incurring. Yes, that's right – teachers were charged for the convenience of being able to put their lunches in a cooled cube or warm up their soup without waiting fifteen of their 30-minute duty-free lunch for the lounge microwave.

Even though rational explanations can be provided for actions like charging teachers for electricity, their impacts remain, and the message is loud and clear. Teachers feel devalued and that their needs and simple conveniences are unimportant. This example isn't limited to Connie's school. Anyone reading this book can likely think of a similar situation. As such, we want to look at appreciation in three categories. One, our decisions as leaders – do they make teachers feel burdened and unappreciated? Two, the circumstances leaders create – do they leave teachers wondering about their value as professionals? Three, the opportunity leaders have – do they intentionally make decisions that demonstrate and reinforce how important teachers are? Tackling each of these categories, decisions, circumstances, and opportunities will send a consistent message that your staff is sure to hear loud and clear.

The Costs Associated With Burdening Our Best

There may not be anything cuter on Earth than a puppy. Whether it's their big "puppy eyes" or their little noses, it's hard not to fall in love with a pup. That said, would you ever consider buying a puppy for someone without checking with them first? Of course, you wouldn't because although puppies are adorable and bring joy, they are a lot of work and can be very destructive. Burdening someone with the responsibility of puppy potty training, the expense of buying food and supplies, and the requirement to be home with the dog as it learns to be independent would be viewed as inconsiderate, irresponsible, and short-sighted.

But, don't we do this to teachers all the time? We might not buy them a puppy, but we give them something of the equivalent. Some of the "opportunities" provided for teachers might be intended to acknowledge how much respect and trust you have in them, but it's often just the burden of being the best. Representing a grade level or department on a committee or chairing a team with a new task may be seen as simply more work rather than an honor or recognition – not always classified as appreciation nor a benefit. Be careful that the "opportunity" to teach a new class or host a family night event are not puppies in disguise, burdening teachers with additional expectations, work, and energy.

Opportunities Disguised As Rewards: Know the Difference

Our superstars tend to be at the top of our "go-to" list when a leadership role is needed. Every school has educators who are consistently responsible, have excellent follow through, and can be depended upon, not only to get a job done but to get it done right. These individuals are repeatedly "rewarded" or in some circumstances, "voluntold" to take on projects that are masked as opportunities beyond their teaching duties.

Worse yet, the 80/20 rule, called the Pareto Principle, is often alive-and-well with the top few teachers doing most of the extra work in a school. This means that 20% of your teachers, the superstars and high backbones, are carrying 80% of the workload. Leaders often ask the same teachers to lead committees, to represent their grade level or department on school or district teams, to organize school-wide events, and more. The teacher who has great rapport with kids and excellent classroom management tends to be assigned to the students with the most challenging behaviors. Their excellence is being tapped into, but the person is not really offered any additional benefits. What kind of "reward" is that?

In the spirit of knowing the impact of our actions, let's take a look at how this plays out for our most valuable teachers. Their gift for being excellent at their job is more work, greater responsibility, bigger challenges, and higher expectations. This translates to less time to maintain the same level of effectiveness. We recognize the need that schools have for these superstars; our schools are better because of them. That's why it's imperative that we learn how to properly show our appreciation.

Requests That Burden

In addition to more work and greater responsibilities, school leaders also have to think carefully about punitive policies that are put into place to address behaviors of a few staff members who likely fall in the mediocre category. Overgeneralized and nonspecific messages that leaders send can do more harm than good. Let's suppose a teacher shows an excessive amount of full-length movies. The leader's response might be to put a new policy into place to discourage this practice by asking all teachers to get prior approval to show a movie. This action only makes superstars jump through additional hoops, taking precious time away from planning and other duties teachers are tasked to accomplish.

Good leaders know they cannot policy their way to better practices. The teachers intended to be impacted by the policy are the least likely to forgo their Friday afternoon reward film, regardless of what you put in writing. Meanwhile, your best teachers scurry to the office to check and make sure that the three-minute clip they showed last week to kick off a new unit wasn't what prompted the new rule.

If you find yourself saying to teachers, "It's not you I'm worried about. There are other teachers who need this boundary" or something similar, take it as a cue that you should re-examine the message you're sending to your best teachers in an effort to manage others. When our requests cause superstars to question themselves, we communicate the polar opposite of our appreciation for them.

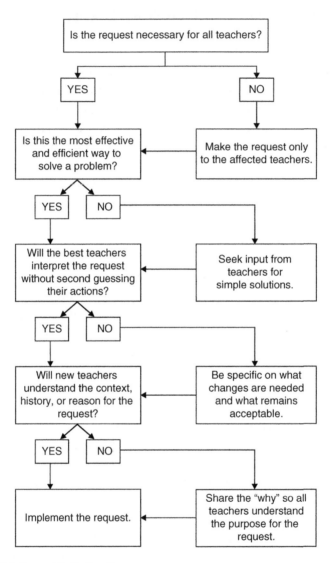

FIGURE 2.1 Request Reflection Process

Before putting out burdensome requests to all teachers, walk yourself through a short reflection process found in Figure 2.1. We offer a series of questions to call attention to the impact that your requests might have on the whole system, particularly your superstars. Start with question one. If the answer is "yes," move on to the second question, and so on. If the answer to any question is "no," look for tips from teachers on how to avoid confusion or the burden of undue pressure that will likely arise for your best teachers.

Developing protocols and practices to help your school run smoothly is vital. We highlight this degree of systems-thinking in our *7 Mindshifts for School Leaders* book (Hamilton, Jones, & Vari, 2023). However, don't use policies to mask an unwillingness to address poor performing teachers. This type of leadership, just like micromanagement, leads to low morale, decreased productivity, poor mental health, and increased turnover (Makinson, 2021). Finding the sweet spot between establishing efficient systems and minimizing the burden they place on teachers is a necessary investment. And, it's the first step in showing your appreciation for the people with the most puppies to raise.

 ## Investment #2: Frame Appreciation With the 4Ws

The hustle-and-bustle of the school day is relentless with very little down time, which is precisely why school leaders need to focus on making rewards and recognition a priority, especially for the hardest working staff members. Common forms of appreciation are pats on the back, buying donuts, or giving weekly shout-outs in the staff memo. Some leaders may even cover a class or duty when they can.

In business, CEOs have the option to offer financial forms of appreciation. This might be a bonus check, an all-expenses paid vacation, or other costly rewards for a job well done. Unfortunately, most schools do not have the luxury or financial freedom for glamorous rewards, but that is no excuse for not rewarding your best teachers with intentional acts of appreciation. According to neuroscience, the brain processes monetary and social rewards in a similar way (Izuma, Saito, & Sadato, 2008). Leaders have the ability to offer and demonstrate appreciation and recognition within the three areas mentioned at the beginning of this chapter: the *decisions* they make, the *circumstances* they create, and the *opportunities* they offer.

Burnout is real and even the best teachers, who seem to have an endless supply of positive energy, are subject to it. According to a Gallup Panel Workforce Study, "four in ten K-12 workers in the U.S. (44%) say they 'always' or 'very often' feel burned out at work, outpacing all other industries nationally" (Marken & Agrawal, 2022). In fact, *Harvard Business Review* states that appreciation in the workplace is the single most impactful influence on employee engagement (Schwartz, 2012). In a time when the demands and strain on teachers is increasing (Hamilton & VanderJagt, 2022.), a small way we can offer a counter narrative is to communicate how important your superstars are to the school, to the students, and to you.

Framing Appreciation

Positive feedback and symbolic methods of appreciation have been proven to increase the feeling of being valued, overall well-being, and levels of motivation (O'Flaherty, Sanders, & Whillans, 2021). A series of studies were conducted to measure non-monetary expressions of appreciation on social workers. The results identify five design features that maximize the impact of the symbolic gestures. They are the messenger, timing, make it public, and details matter (O'Flaherty, Sanders, & Whillans, 2021). We have applied these factors in a 4Ws Model, shown in Figure 2.2,

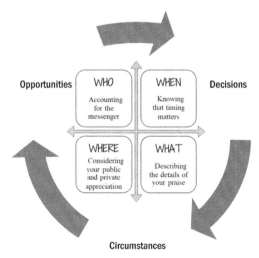

FIGURE 2.2

to highlight considerations for you to explore before you deliver your appreciation. All of these are conscious and explicit decisions that school leaders can make, circumstances they can create, and opportunities they can manage. Your best teachers deserve your attention and appreciation in these ways.

Who – Accounting for the Messenger

Yes, as the school leader your opinion matters, but it isn't the only one in the school. Great school leaders find ways to increase the number of messengers giving appreciation and sending positive messages. Teachers receive positive and negative feedback from a variety of sources. Sometimes, your accolades might be needed to neutralize a criticism of a teacher, but, in any event, the person who delivers the message is one of the most important details.

Consider the numerous groups of people who influence how our best teachers view themselves. They often get positive affirmations from their students, but if a teacher is focused on a parent who is upset about their child's latest grade, it can eclipse the good. In these types of circumstances, it is beneficial to remind your superstars of the recent praise they received by their students or the wonderful impact they have from year-to-year. If a local news article unfairly represents teachers and the profession, you may counter such negativity by soliciting recognition or thanks from your Board of Education instead of you. Whenever teachers get granular with a negative response to their work, it's critical that leaders zoom out to the big picture so that teachers stay focused on their incredible impact.

Another powerful group who lift teachers is their colleagues. Great school leaders encourage peer-to-peer gratitude and build systems for doing so. When coworkers acknowledge one another it boosts working relationships and promotes team spirit (Rabha, 2023). Opening a staff meeting with an opportunity for teachers to give a shout-out to someone else brings meaning to their work. While this is a predictable pattern and acknowledgements are most effective when they are unexpected, systematic feedback builds a culture of affirmation and gratitude. The idea is to open the door for genuine thank yous, not going around the room and forcing each person to say something nice about someone else.

The strategies and methods that your best teachers use every day are examples that you probably point to when providing detailed feedback to other teachers. If a tip about how to build movement into a lesson or technology tool used to increase student engagement was inspiration for a suggestion you make to another teacher, take the time to communicate to your superstar that you shared their tool or strategy with someone else. It's less important that you name the superstar to the teacher receiving the idea and more about letting your best teachers know that you appreciate their talents so much that you're making an effort to share them widely.

As leaders, we have to capitalize on every opportunity to share good news. When you receive a compliment from a student's family member, praising a teacher for their collaboration, share your enthusiasm with the news, then encourage the family member to communicate their experience with the teacher directly. Make it easy for them to offer their appreciation by giving them a voicemail number, an email address, or letting them know that the teacher is working the ticket booth at the basketball game on Thursday – an incredible time to make the teacher's day. This brings us to timing.

When – Knowing That Timing Matters

Another consideration when showing appreciation is timing. There is the immediacy of acknowledging an act when it happens or shortly thereafter. You should also determine times of the day, week, semester, or school year when a reminder of a teacher's value is needed. Here are some points in time when intentionally giving appreciation is valuable:

- ◆ The beginning or end of a marking period.
- ◆ Right before or after conference night.
- ◆ Monday morning at the start of a workweek.
- ◆ When a challenge is faced.
- ◆ During a window of time when state assessments are given.
- ◆ In the summer when they might be in a different state of mind.
- ◆ As they enter the building in the morning.
- ◆ After a challenging class period.

- ◆ During their planning time.
- ◆ In a long stretch between breaks in the calendar.
- ◆ On full moon days.
- ◆ Right before, during, or after a holiday season.
- ◆ When a department or grade level meets.
- ◆ Anytime there seems to be a slump.
- ◆ A week or so after an initial "thanks" to reinforce it's still valued.

As we've said, making appreciation a priority requires leaders to think about systems for doing so and the proper timing of those systems. Just like random impromptu questioning isn't likely to garner high levels of cognitive demand for students, unplanned appreciation is not likely to create a culture that values it. Appreciating others is a muscle, and to do so off-the-cuff with ease is only built and embedded within systems and structures that exist for praising within predetermined timelines. Appreciation should also be planned so that it can be public.

Be careful not to take the efforts of your best teachers for granted. The show of effort to extend gratitude or appreciation is more likely to be noticed by your best teachers. Qualify your words with something like, "I've been wanting to tell you…" or "I continue to notice how you always…" If a teacher is known for staying outside until the last bus leaves the school parking lot, these types of above-and-beyond actions are not too small to be acknowledged and appreciated.

Where – Considering Your Public and Private Settings

It's important to consider the audience for positive feedback and expressions of gratitude. Public acknowledgement of appreciation can elevate the boost, but in some cases it can spark comparisons that have a negative impact on your team. Too much attention on your superstars can cause your other teachers to believe there is favoritism, which is not a mindset you want to foster. You want to strike a balance of public gratitude and private praise for their accolades.

Take into consideration how private the individual is, whether the public display will instill motivation or competition, and how those not receiving the attention will respond. We suggest asking each employee their preference. If you already have a question-naire for these types of things, add to it this question:

When I do something that is noteworthy, I prefer to accept appreciation in the following way(s):

 a. Publicly in person
 b. Privately in person
 c. Publicly via email or newsletter
 d. Privately via email or messaging
 e. I'm happy to be praised in any format

Sometimes a simple nod of appreciation is all it takes, such as "Mr. Jacobs, the photos you posted of your students' projects are impressive. Thanks for sharing them on the Facebook page. It means a lot to our families when they get to see their kids in action. It looks great." This is quick, specific, and meaningful. The positive impact may not only feel great for Mr. Jacobs. As he is publicly honored for his effort, other members of your team will learn about the positive activities going on at the school, demon-strating the great culture in which they work and inspiring them to contribute in unique ways as well. And, you just might find more promotional posts on your social media after your public kudos. More about this in the next chapter.

What – Describing the Details

Lack of specificity about how the appreciation was inspired also makes it less impactful. Sure, it's nice to hear "good job," but it's flat and generic. Offer organic appreciation that is spe-cific and meaningful. If your efforts to boost your teachers are monotonous, they lack genuineness. This leads to people questioning your sincerity and does little to build trust and rapport. Share details that describe what was done to deserve recognition and how it impacted others in a positive way. We'll provide you with a model for praising well in Chapter 9. Now, just know that details matter. Your old "way to go" comment is not resonating unless you describe what you appreciate so much.

Now that you're thinking about the 4Ws of who (account for the messenger), when (knowing that timing matters), where (considering public or private settings), and what (describing the details), you're reading to move into how. So far, we've focused on thinking about what to *say* when you share your appreciation for teachers. The other powerful consideration for whether your message is well received is *how* you communicate it – and it's not always through your actual words.

Maximizing Your Investment: Understand Love Languages

Showing appreciation is part of what successful leaders do, and most of the time, it doesn't take much effort. Signals of praise such as public acknowledgement for a specific contribution or a peer who is willing to help a busy co-worker to count field trip money are a couple of examples of simple ways we can build a culture of gratitude. It's important to make the effort to communicate "I see and value you." It's equally important to consider how you share this message with them.

In their book, *The 5 Languages of Appreciation in the Workplace* (2012), Gary Chapman and Paul White warn us that while we might think our co-workers know these gestures are our way of appreciating them, there are five specific "languages" that your teachers will value more than others when receiving a message of appreciation or encouragement. This is critical because if you are recognizing someone and demonstrating appreciation in a "language" that they don't connect with, it will not have the positive impact that you intend for it to have.

An example of when there is misalignment between a teacher's preferred language of appreciation and the method you're using to show gratitude would be when your efforts cause a teacher to think "it's great that my principal gives me a high five almost every day, but it would be nice if she would show some interest in what I learned at the conference that I recently attended." Sound familiar?

This is a mismatch in love languages; the teacher values quality time over physical touch. The difference is they would prefer

60 seconds of one-on-one dialogue and you're trying to build culture with a high five. It's important to note that we often show appreciation in the manner that we like to receive it. Knowing this requires school leaders to get to know their teachers and their preferred method for receiving appreciation.

Otherwise, the principal risks getting a false sense that a teacher knows how much they are appreciated, the last thing that you want for any teacher. In order to maximize the impact of your time and energy (and sometimes money) you should provide gratitude using the different languages of appreciation that Chapman and White shared in their book (2012). In addition to understanding more about your teachers' love languages, you should also try to vary your approach when planning events for the whole staff to increase the odds of your message translating strongly.

We have provided some examples of how you can maximize your actions in Figure 2.3.

How the 4Ws Profits the Whole System

The 4Ws Model provides a system for appreciation that makes it more purposeful and less random. When school leaders consider the who, what, where, and when, they're more likely to offer appreciation in a way that includes everyone. You might otherwise miss a person, and you don't want that person to be one of your best teachers. Systematizing appreciation and making it a daily priority will boost morale, benefiting all of your teachers as you work to ensure that your best teachers feel what they deserve to feel at work.

That said, we can apply the 4Ws Model to our call-to-action that you treat every week as Teacher Appreciation Week. It takes a little work at the beginning of the school year, but it pays off in a greater sense of belonging and higher levels of morale throughout the rest of the school year. Let's take a look at how you can do this in the future.

Making Every Week Teacher Appreciation Week

At the beginning of the school year, teachers take time to get to know their students. Learning student dispositions through organized ice breakers, questions, and activities give teachers

Languages of Appreciation		
	EXAMPLES	**AVOID**
Acts of Service	• Schedule a volunteer to assist staff with clerical tasks like copies or preparation of materials. • Fast track tech or custodial support when something isn't working. • Ask "How can I help?" before helping. • Provide templates or clear guidelines to make tasks simpler.	• Offering to help, then not following through. • Completing a task the way you would, instead of how they want it.
Physical Touch	• "Secret" handshakes. • Fist pumps. • High fives. • Hugs when welcomed (especially in emotional moments). • Honor individual boundaries and cultural norms.	• Invading personal space. • Lack of consideration for cultural differences. • Making assumptions about what is welcomed.
Quality Time	• Stop by and check in. • Coordinate social events. • Initiate conversation to show interest in their lives. • Follow up after conversations or events for ongoing connection. • Close your laptop, silence your phone, and delay responding to interruptions. • Choose meeting times that are convenient for the teacher.	• Giving someone or something else your time and attention instead of the teacher or their needs. • Interruptions when you're with this person. • Disregard for infringement on quality time with loved ones outside school.
Tangible Gifts	• Small tokens that reflect an interest or hobby of the teacher. • School supplies or tools that the teacher mentions or that you notice might be needed. • Favorite foods or drinks. • Explain why a gift or treat was specifically chosen for them.	• Generic or impersonal items. • Giving too many or too costly gifts that are not valued.
Words of Affirmation	• Take time to acknowledge someone by name in a staff meeting for something specific. • Put a handwritten note in a teacher's mailbox, on their desk, or mail to their home. • Give credit where credit is due. • Choose semantics carefully.	• Sarcastic comments, even in jest. • Public criticism. • Careless use of semantics.

FIGURE 2.3 Languages of Appreciation

incredible insight about students' interests and likes. Those who are successful in using this information build meaningful connections with their students and develop a culture of compassion in the classroom. They often also have fewer behavior problems and students put more effort into their learning. We cannot overstate: Relationships. Relationships. Relationships.

Leaders can use this same strategy to get to know their teachers. What motivates them? What are they passionate about? What interests do they have? Beyond building rapport with your staff, this information allows you to personalize your appreciation and celebrate their value all year long by making every week Teacher Appreciation Week.

The first full week in May is named Teacher Appreciation Week. Schools everywhere use these days to elevate teachers and show gratitude for their work. Leaders find sponsors to provide lunches, solicit PTO members to share words of thanks, or create schedules that provide extended breaks for teachers. All kinds of creative efforts are made to celebrate this week and make teachers feel special.

If the other 35 weeks of the year aren't also focused on a culture of appreciation and value, then Teacher Appreciation Week will only lift spirits temporarily. The five days of feeling good slips back to the status quo of feeling undervalued or, worse yet, ignored and unappreciated. This truth is evidenced by realities in the corporate world as well.

Studies showed that the most successful teams had an average positivity ratio of 5.6 positive expressions for every single negative one (Losada & Heaphy, 2004). We don't think it is a coincidence that this proportion aligns to what we are told about Positive Behavior Interventions and Supports (PBIS) where a 5:1 ratio of confirmations, praise, and approvals are offered for every criticism or disparagement (Cook et al., 2017).

Let's return to what teachers do to build classroom culture at the beginning of the school year – they get to know their students' interests, preferences, and perspectives. You can do the same using our 4Ws approach. Develop a quick survey with questions like the ones below or download ours. Note that they follow the who, when, where, and what format. We mentioned the use of a survey to onboard teachers, but imagine using a similar set of questions each year for each teacher regarding their ideas about staff appreciation.

When I do something that's worthy of appreciation, I value hearing most from:

a. Students
b. Parents
c. Other staff members
d. Principals and supervisors
e. Other _____

When I do something that is noteworthy, appreciation means the most to me when it is offered:

a. When I'm willing to take on a challenge, but before it starts
b. After I've achieved success
c. As a reminder to boost me up when times are challenging
d. During a planned event like a luncheon or staff meeting
e. I'm always ready to be appreciated

When I do something that is noteworthy, I prefer to accept appreciation in the following way(s):

a. Publicly in person
b. Privately in person
c. Publicly via email or newsletter
d. Privately via email or messaging
e. I'm happy to be praised in any format

Which aspects of your work do you value appreciation for most:

a. The contributions I make to our team, grade level, content area
b. My impact as a classroom teacher
c. The extra assignments or leadership positions I hold
d. The small things that I do that most people don't see
e. Other _____

I'm motivated most by (rank order for yourself):

1. Helping me with my day-to-day tasks or providing me with more time to get my work done during the day
2. Fist pumps, high fives, and motivators of that kind
3. Time and attention to connect and discuss progress individually
4. A personalized and thoughtful gift from someone
5. Affirmation that I'm on the right track

A quick survey of this kind at the beginning of the year will help you to understand more about teacher motivation so that you can personalize your appreciation using the 4Ws and your understanding of the five love languages that we described in the last section. Making appreciation a priority will demonstrate to your best teachers that you care deeply about them as people, not just the work they do, and it will elevate the spirits of the whole staff as you make teacher appreciation a weekly endeavor, not just one week of the year.

The survey itself can be a boost to staff. Teachers will look forward to seeing how the results are used. Therefore, not following through with the results can build resentment. As Todd has shared, leadership is not an event (Whitaker, 2020.) and the follow through or lack thereof can strengthen or damage the best of intentions.

The Bottom Line

Staff members who feel appreciated by their principals are more aware of the value they bring to the school system. Too often our best teachers are recognized for their efforts with what seems like a privilege or honor, but in reality is simply a larger burden on their already full plates. Effective school leaders consider a framework for showing appreciation that takes into account the most appropriate source to communicate the praise, the ideal timing that will make the most impact, whether the gratitude will be shared publicly or privately, and they include details of exactly what they appreciate.

This framework for offering gratitude ensures that the appreciation you have for all that your teachers do is received in a manner that is impactful. A systematic approach to expressing gratitude to your superstars prevents them from falling through the cracks, going unnoticed, and feeling like they are taken for granted. While it might sound like we're adding more to your plate, the five methods for showing appreciation often do not require much effort once you're aware of them.

Circle back to the story shared at the beginning of this chapter. The decisions we make, no matter how small or trivial they may appear, can have incredible effects on your staff. A single gesture like allowing teachers the convenience of having appliances in their classrooms can hit many different languages of appreciation. It limits wasted time going back-and-forth to a central location for coffee, snacks, etc. A statement affirming the value of teachers is worth providing them this minor convenience, and being able to brew a cup of coffee in the classroom saves them time and money because they can skip the coffee house drive-thru each morning.

HOW TO MAKE YOUR INITIAL DEPOSIT

You can jump right in to expanding the way you think about and share appreciation by inviting your staff to take a Love Language Assessment. In just a few minutes, they can find a quick online assessment and get their results. Give them time to have fun with learning about the different methods of appreciation, then collect a summary. A Google form for teachers to individually input their results or a single page chart where their names can be added under the heading of physical touch, acts of service, quality time, gifts or words of affirmation. Now, you'll have a snapshot of your entire staff along with the option to look at an individual's preferred method of appreciation.

3

Going Beyond Business Cards

A Hashtag That Works

For years schools have recognized student achievement in a variety of ways from National Honor Society Induction to student of the month certificates. Whether achievements on the field or in the classroom, student success is a hallmark of excellence. However, too often these accomplishments remain known to those within the walls of a school and nothing further than the schoolyard is publicized. We have to begin to purposefully include the greater school community, and the reasons are endless – reputation, recruitment, pride, publicity, relationships. Add to the list. This is precisely why Joe and his team met.

With a desire to showcase the outstanding partnerships and cooperative work within the New Castle County Vocational-Technical School District (NCCVT), Joe sat with the school's cooperative employment coordinators to discuss how each school and the district could effectively showcase the tremendous work that was being done by students in partnership with local businesses. The community tangentially knew that the students worked outside of the school walls but definitely not to the extent that the students were being employed by partners, contributing to the local economy.

With a goal of featuring students who are actively employed, recognizing and thanking over 400 business partners, showcasing the best teachers, and generating excitement for potential student/

DOI: 10.4324/9781003321316-3

business relationships, the team brainstormed a ton of ideas. Too often they heard, "oh, you guys are the best kept secret" (referring to the school system) and that was a perception they wanted to change. For the benefit of students and the community, they wanted to be included in positive conversation within households, among businesses, with legislators, and in the community in general.

The district is poised for workforce development, and they wanted to be seen as such. The team thought about enhancing the school website, expanding their social media reach, and considered other potential platforms. They weren't short of ideas, but everything seemed too generic. They certainly weren't marketers, and school leaders are still mostly new to the concept of schools having brand identities.

As the group sat around the table, Joe started throwing out ideas about creating a hashtag for the district with the notion that the district could start anchoring ideas, photos, and events to a particular hashtag that would resonate with the community and make it easy to follow. Twitter was starting to become more popular within education, and Joe was beginning to recognize the power of this online community. Regardless, the team consisted of mostly social media novices, but they did see the importance of a singular hashtag to embody what was being done by our best people, inside and outside of the organization.

As the team bounced ideas around, #NCCVTWorks was born. With the district's mission being: To provide superior Career and Technical Education enabling all students to achieve their aspirations, #NCCVTWorks was perfect. The hashtag included four key aspects of the district's priorities. One, it sent the message that the district was working and working well for its students, families, and community. Data, pictures, and events could all be pushed out with the hashtag, reinforcing the great work being accomplished.

Two, being a vocational technical district, it reinforced that working was a key aspect of a student's senior year experience. The co-op program is a critical component due to the on-the-job-training that students simply can't experience in a classroom. This effort is a key driver for workforce development.

Three, it allowed for versatility to look back on graduates and the impact they are having on the community. Whether working in a hospital or starting their own electrical company, many graduates went into the industry they studied and were productive and active citizens.

Four, the hashtag could be used by anyone. This allows the District leaders to post about the best teachers along with all of what the co-op program offers to students and graduates. It also allows anyone who sees something that is worthy of sharing to post and use #NCCVTWorks for anyone following the hashtag on social media.

The result was clear. The team discovered a great hashtag that is now commonly used as part of the district's messaging. Rarely are posts present on social media platforms without the #NCCVTWorks hashtag. Now, more people know about the tremendous impact that the district has, and, guess what, the hashtag works.

This example was of a vocational school but an elementary school can accomplish the same thing. Sharing your successes is fun when you don't need a boost but imperative when you do. You may have someone whose dream is to be an influencer on Tik-Tok but managing the vlogging section of the school's website is where they can start. Maybe one class records a short video (and by short it could be 30 seconds) and shares one per day on your website. Then, expand your exposure by posting on social media sites like Instagram with your school hashtag #ParkviewPride. And rather than the teacher posting the videos, have a student-of-the-day do the honors. This also allows the families at home to stop asking their children, "What did you do at school today?" The typical answer to this question is "Nothing." Instead, families can visit the website at night or scroll through the hashtag and ask their child questions about their class, grade level, or something interesting that they find.

The Costs Associated With Inconsistent and Intermittent Digital Media Presence

In an ever-increasing digital world, you would think that business cards are irrelevant. That may be true if you never planned on leaving the house again to attend a business function, but business cards are still very useful. Depending on the circumstances, they allow for a quick exchange of critical information with the understanding that a follow-up call or email is perfectly fine. A well-crafted business card not only has useful information, but it also communicates the brand of the company. The card often represents the beginning of a relationship, a launch to something greater. The power of distributing or accepting a card is the understanding that it may lead to something more – an important business connection, a partnership, or maybe just lunch. The exchange represents a continuation of the relationship with the hope that it eventually benefits both individuals.

This is where great schools can embrace the idea of business cards and their purpose. Let's be real, though, most teachers don't have business card (but there is no reason we do not provide them). Administrators do, but even they may not use them very well. In professional education circles, events like product launches, business mixers, or rotary breakfasts aren't common. Therein lies the challenge. Education is focused within the system – primarily on teaching and learning – and not necessarily on elements outside of the system. However, the outside elements can positively or negatively affect a school, which is why marketing and branding are both paramount.

Rather than succumb to negativity, schools must accept this responsibility to share the good things that are happening all the time. Moving beyond the business card entails understanding branding and how schools can leverage multiple mediums to showcase and highlight their impact. The most important reason to tell your school's story is so that you can control or contribute to the narrative; if you don't, someone else will. They always will. And, unfortunately, it's usually not favorable news.

Schools can learn a lot from businesses, including paying close attention to how the school and district are viewed by the public. If a business fails to attend to public perception, it dies. If schools do, their reputations suffer. Thinking this way helps schools move from being a commodity to having a brand identity – "a commodity (that can be easily substituted) or a brand (that has a distinctive set of features and benefits that cannot easily be replaced)" (Kim & Choi, 2022).

Imagine a new teacher luncheon or visit to a local diner. Arrange it so when the teachers arrive, they find a school shirt, a drink tumbler with the mascot on it, and a stack of business cards waiting at their seat. This can be a simple tradition of welcoming new teachers into your school team. Before you know it, veteran teachers will be greeting your lunch guests when they return to school and share their memories of when they enjoyed their inaugural luncheon.

Schools may not always fully embrace the need to brand themselves, but COVID19, among other factors, inflated the need. In a time of growing competition among schools and the way instruction can be delivered, schools should take a close look at themselves and how they are connecting with the community. If not, they may soon find themselves with empty desks in unoccupied classrooms, which is already occurring in some districts and states across the country.

One aspect of schooling that is not featured enough in the press is the amazing classroom teachers we have and the exemplary work being done by them. Schools typically feature progressive Science, Technology, Engineering, Arts, and Math (STEAM) programs or state-of-the-art Career and Technical Education pathways or an incredible athletic program, but rarely are the faculty or what's going on inside the classroom showcased. This is something that school leaders might ignore to their detriment. Teachers are known by their students, and some of the parents, but maybe not beyond them. Schools may lack a concerted effort to build the identity and academic prowess of the school by championing and highlighting the wonderful faculty and all their gifts and talents.

That said, some private and public schools and universities do this exceptionally well. And others not so much. The more successful marketers tout their teachers or professors and their expertise. They highlight their backgrounds through faculty pages that feature their degrees, experience, and accolades. They feature photos of happy children joyfully learning from their beloved teachers. With family mobility all schools potentially exist in a competitive environment thus marketing must be a key aspect of the school. If someone is to make an informed decision on where to send their child to school, they look for the best. Many schools can learn from the most well-marketed schools in this area.

Hopefully all universities understand that they are viewed, by those who attend them, as a threshold to a better life by obtaining a superior education. The general assumption made by parents is often that the more impressive the staff is, the more the students will learn and be prepared. We are not going to discuss the merits of that narrative, but we can't overlook how higher education has pushed their story successfully. To a great degree, they often focus on their instructors as the lure. All K-12 schools can do the same.

It begins, though, by embracing the business card mentality – the school has something to offer students, their families, and its community that no one else can propose and that the school is not just a commodity that is easily replaced. By focusing a large part of our brand on our best teachers, we celebrate them while spotlighting a major point of pride.

Another factor that schools may have to contend with beyond choice and increased competition is the negative narrative toward public schools. Much of this "glass half empty" view has to do with how people think and how they process their environment. The work of Dr. Martin Seligman powerfully demonstrates how some humans are "wired" to be pessimistic (Skipper, 2018). His work identifies how we are designed to protect ourselves and how we shouldn't get too comfortable because things can change quickly, and not always for the better. History has taught us to live this way.

Therefore, it's even more important for us to work to influence the narrative highlighting the positives that might easily go unnoticed. Make friends with your local reporters. Invite them to events that are points of pride for your school. We've even been known to draft articles to increase the chance that they'll be published to offset any unflattering perceptions that people might have picked up through the rumor mill. At times it seems that the media (and misinformation shared on social channels) add to this negative dynamic.

As the old saying goes, "if it bleeds, it leads." Our brains are attracted to negative inputs and controversy sells. What's startling is a Pew Research Center study that revealed that most people believe that the media negatively contributes to our view of the world, yet, we still tune in to follow the hype (Auxier, 2020). Schools are doing tremendous things each day, and because educators may be fighting a negative narrative in the news or social media, it is essential that we share our message, consistently and pervasively. We all know that there is always work to be done in our schools to ensure the achievement of all students. And every leader is aware their school has its challenges. However, educating youth is not easy, which is why we need the best people to move forward with us.

Luckily all schools have accomplishments to be proud of, which is why we have many bright spots to share. If other people are going to promote bad things then we must work to inform everyone of our many successes. This active approach denotes the school's responsibility to promote themselves as a brand.

The question is how to do this well. How should schools take steps to brand themselves properly within the market? Because people at times make assumptions about schools based on their own experiences, featuring quality teachers is the first best step. It builds the identity of the school beyond just the brick and mortar of its exterior walls.

As schools highlight and recognize teachers and students, onlookers can see the real people working inside of them, doing incredible things for kids. People care about people. Programs are great and can also be included, but the connection to the school is made in the stories we tell. Let's look at what schools could be doing and how, in particular for our superstar teachers whose stories are the first we want to point to when we're ready to build the brand. Keep passing out the business cards, but we have to go beyond that for our brand to matter and for our best teachers to have their stories told.

Investment #3: Brand Using the S.P.A. Treatment

Effective school leaders embrace the responsibility of building a school brand and using resources to do it well. From the outset, we want to clearly identify what branding is and what it is not.

For branding efforts to be successful, schools must open a door to what is occurring within the school and share it in a variety of ways, using multiple methods and platforms. It's not just about pushing out routine information or posting mindless tweets. Good school branding builds and reinforces the identity of the school through messaging, providing the audience with an experience. Each piece of information shared is a brush stroke of the school's purpose and impact, slowly developing the characteristics of the school on an open canvas. This is a picture being continuously painted, constantly piquing the interest of the community in new and engaging ways.

The school's vision, mission, core values, and culture should be evident in what is messaged to the public, not simply the words but the photos representing the people, the data revealing the accomplishments, and the testimonials reinforcing the outcomes. The school culture should unveil itself through branding. We are not referring to promotional efforts for promotion's sake, but rather providing the community with real information about the great things happening that are all tied to student success.

We would be remiss if we didn't acknowledge that if your school is failing and not successful, no amount of branding or promotion will change the narrative. For those schools, the internal work must be done first. However, there is no reason why an improvement-focused story can't be told. Don't be afraid to look for the good parts, even if you have to squint. Start there while you add and develop other shining successes. Letting the community know where you are going, how you're going to get there, and the best teachers who are ready and able to do the work are key steps to changing their minds and may even compel others to help with the transformation. There is nothing wrong with informing the community, letting them know that the work is uphill but underway. Sometimes it is more fun to mow where the grass is long. The investment that you're making in your brand is also an investment in your best teachers. To depict how this works and what school leaders can do to lift their reputation to new heights, we apply our S.P.A. treatment, beginning with our best teachers in the school.

Of course, you must be aware that your brand consists of everyone – the work that everyone is doing must be showcased in one way or another. But, we build brands with our best foot forward using our best teachers' work. When we tell their stories and when their stories are connected with the school's priorities, we begin to attract even more "best" teachers to our school. Let's take a look at how the cycle works.

Stories + Priorities = Attraction

To ensure that you follow a solid prescription for effective branding, we created a simple equation for schools: Stories + Priorities = Attraction. This process, shown in Figure 3.1, is simple, and yet it has the capability of making a total difference for what people think about and how they feel about your school.

Stories

Let's begin with your story. In *The Power of Branding* (2015), Sinanis and Sanfelippo address the importance for schools to tell their story and share the tremendous things happening each and every day. We've already established that too often, the local community, and sometimes parents, don't know the great work occurring within a school. One truth that all school leaders must accept is that technology and various social media platforms have transformed how people learn about the news. Accepting this is critical because when something unfortunate happens in the school or elsewhere, it will be advertised and shared quickly

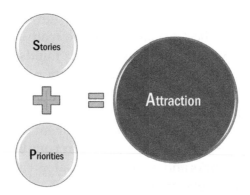

FIGURE 3.1

and repeatedly on social channels. The major challenge is that when a school earns a reputation – good or bad, true or untrue – it is very hard to change. Everyone wants to associate with a winner. With sports teams there is a record regarding wins and losses. As a school when we share enough wins, people start to lose sight of other things that we are still working on. There may be some negative voices that you cannot control, but you can make sure that you have a loud and powerful voice that is difficult to overlook.

Joe recalls a very telling scenario about how people form opinions about schools. One summer his sons participated on the local swim team and a man he was standing next to started a casual conversation. Before long, the man asked Joe what he did for a living. Joe told him he was an administrator and the school where he worked. The man immediately grimaced and said, "wow, that is a tough school." Joe asked the gentleman how he knew about the school and he indicated that his buddy used to teach there. Surprised, Joe asked who and the gentlemen stated that "oh, you wouldn't know him, he worked there in the early 80s." Mind you, Joe had this conversation in 2008, almost 25 years later.

Unfortunately, people hang onto the information that they have and rarely question its truthfulness, even years after their encounter. At the time, the school where Joe was working was receiving tons of awards and accolades. The problem was that only the people who knew about the good news were also working at the school. It is our responsibility as school leaders to help inform the greater community of new and relevant news through multiple avenues and channels.

The stories told should feature the staff and students, especially the impact of our best teachers. When it comes to schools, people want to know the impact. Impact sells because it's emotional, interesting, and newsworthy. It's easy to feature the athletic teams, the band, the school plays, etc. But, lifting the brand of the school requires stories about our best people and the work they're doing that impacts the community.

Highlighting our best teachers will not only sell the school's story, but it will also positively influence the morale of the staff, sending a message that we're proud of our accomplishments. This demonstrates how much our best teachers are valued. Consider Teacher Appreciation Week: it's a great example of too little too late in the year, especially for storytelling. All throughout the year, there should be educator spotlights, highlighting stories about the best of the best of our teaching staff. The spotlight should entail an action shot of them engaged with their class, their name, the grade or subject(s) they teach, some of their history and path to the classroom, their degree or degrees, other credentials, and any other notable information (see Figure 3.2).

You're not alienating your mediocre or backbone teachers as you lift the best. The opposite is true. You're building the reputation of your best teachers and just that – the best examples you have of what we're proudest of and how we want to be represented in the media. This works to provide a model for all other teachers, and your best teachers deserve to be front-and-center in the news.

The goal is to build the educational stature of the best teachers and showcase them as the superstars that they are. This achieves several goals. First, it highlights staff and their impact; second, it provides insight into what happens in classrooms day-in and day-out; third, it creates a collective identity of the school from a personal level, telling the story of our best work; fourth, as the branding efforts grow, it provides the foundation for highlighting the staff so that people have a frame of reference that builds the story even further; fifth, it lets the greater community know where their tax contributions are going. These days, schools have a unique opportunity to leverage social media and new platforms in ways that can fundamentally change how people learn about a school and its brand. Telling the story of our best teachers is the first aspect of our S.P.A. treatment that goes beyond giving them business cards to hand out. But, it doesn't complete the cycle; you have to connect the stories to the school's priorities for the impact to matter as you build the brand.

Priorities

Some schools with great reputations earn that reputation by systematically telling the story of every great moment, program,

FIGURE 3.2

initiative, and circumstance. This is why "priorities" is the second component of the cycle. It is also critical not to overcomplicate this part. Consider a school's strategic plan and the associated priorities. Many schools are focused on recruiting and retaining high quality teachers. Providing data and insights into a school's recruiting campaign and informing them about the great people on staff is an active way to demonstrate what the school is doing that is attracting and retaining the very best. When we show our best at their best, we're demonstrating our commitment to the plan.

Schools are beginning to create highlight reels with aerial drone footage of the school, all in an effort to attract teachers. These videos should not be isolated to the timeline of job fairs. Instead, parents and the community should be privy to them. We acknowledge that opening the school doors to this degree of information sharing creates a level of vulnerability for schools and teachers. However, it's worth it. The more the community is informed, the less chance there is that they will hear and listen to a false narrative. We want them, instead, to know the story of our best teachers, creating almost a celebrity status for them, which is exactly what universities are doing with professors as we described above.

The story we tell about our best teachers, connected to the priorities we set, builds the brand that the school and the teachers deserve. That's why we call it the S.P.A. treatment. When people see and hear about the impact of their local public schools, and teachers can relish in the pride they feel about the work they do, we're making an investment that tells everyone what we value, and that cycle only continues to attract the teachers who we want to join the team.

Attraction

The power in the cycle is what it yields, which is attraction. Attracting students and more superstar staff members is multifaceted, from students who may choose to attend your school (if that is an option), to prospective teachers who may want to work in your school, to business partners who want to support your efforts, to legislators who work with administrators on initiatives. The equation (stories + priorities = attraction) magnetizes the school and attracts the positive attention that you want. You're telling the story of your best teachers, and you're attracting others who want to join the team because of what they see.

People want to be part of something that has an impact and that elevates the status of the people who are making that impact. All you need to make this happen is to start to build your army of branders.

🔒🔒 Maximizing Your Investment: Build an Army of Branders

Creating the narrative for your school, and continually building and reinforcing it, is no easy task. Originally, many schools allowed social media efforts to be organic, guided loosely by an acceptable use policy, and mainly open for those staff members who were inclined to delve into the social media world. Most schools chalked this up as a nice thing to do but not as an essential school function. As we've identified, telling your story and contributing to the narrative through social media is a must do because it is a robust way to reach vast and diverse audiences.

To take advantage of the various platforms, schools must build an infrastructure in three ways. First, every school should have someone who will take the lead on branding and take responsibility for website accuracy, updates, and social media posts. This individual can run professional learning on the various platforms, how to create meaningful posts, and what are appropriate and inappropriate things to share. Essentially, they are the go-to person for branding in the school. In fact, if money is available, this should be a stipend position, almost like a school's own Public Information Officer. That said, one person is not enough; this person is serving as the guide and resident expert for applying the S.P.A. treatment.

The second way schools can do this successfully is by building an army of branders. These are individuals who are willing to enter the branding game. The army is willing to post, repost, and comment as frequently as possible. They willingly generate activity around posts. This larger group process cannot be understated. It's great to have a principal or a teacher who is active, posting wonderful pictures and captions. However, for branding purposes – reaching large audiences, reinforcing the school's message, and providing highlights – an army is necessary.

Their activity builds the necessary momentum and digital footprint. Think about parents, community members, clerical staff, and other supporters who can come together in this regard. Be mindful to work with this community of branders so they are clear on the messaging and its intent. The last thing you want is for this to become unwieldy and something that has to be managed. However, with the right community and with everyone knowing the purpose of the efforts this can become a great way to share the wonderful things happening from multiple people.

The third key to your branding initiative is to have a well-developed branding calendar. The tough thing about telling your story is that it requires a consistent and dogged approach. Too often, we fall into the "is this good enough to post?" trap. If it's about the positive impact of a teacher or a positive outcome for a student, share it and share it widely. Do not waste time debating the value of a post. A well-developed calendar to guide posts can help eliminate mental posting blocks. Figure 3.3 illustrates what a few days could look like.

Lastly, have fun with this endeavor. Create activities like committing to a ten-day social media challenge of telling your story. It only takes a few minutes a day to post on multiple social media platforms. If your community is active on Facebook, Instagram, or TikTok, you can share a pic, or create a quick video and post on all three sites. For ten straight days, commit to communicating

Sunday	Monday	Tuesday	Wednesday	Thursday	Friday	Saturday
	Inspirational Post	Teacher Tip	Wednesday Wow	Extra-Curricular Activity Spotlight	School Good News	School Activity Feature
	Educator Spotlight	Alumni Shout Out	Student Activity (e.g. lab)	Retweet	Update on a school initiative	School Activity Feature
	Motivation Monday	Family Fun Activities	Wednesday Wow	Teacher Shout Out	Staff Spotlight	School Activity Feature
	Inside the classroom	Educator Spotlight	Student Activity (e.g. art)	Staff Spotlight	School Good News	School Activity Feature

FIGURE 3.3

something special about your most valuable teachers. Keep in mind that teachers who are outside the superstar status might be the best branders, and if they are truly talented in this area, they can quickly become irreplaceable. Sometimes what makes teachers "the best" is a contribution that they make to the school beyond the classroom.

The Stories + Priorities = Attraction equation works and will lift the entire system.

⚮⚮ How the S.P.A. Treatment Profits the Whole System

A fun pastime among sports enthusiasts is to debate the best sports teams of all time. Undoubtedly, this is a futile exercise as fierce loyalties and subjective opinions cloud objective judgment. Regardless, there are some heavy hitters that always make the list that can't be ignored. Who could argue that the '98 Yankees definitely stand out? From the batter's box to the pitching mound, they dominated the playing field. In the 90s, the Chicago Bulls were incredible, while the Edmonton Oilers in the 80s were unstoppable.

The question that looms when these arguments arise is about the essence of what it means to achieve unmistakable greatness. Putting together a winning team is far more complex than just assembling talented people. Players need to not only be the very best in their particular position, but also must complement the team as a whole. The great teams at which we marvel always possess incredible dynamics among the players and coaches that transcend talent. Teamwork truly does make the dream work.

Although schools aren't vying for NBA championships, and certainly won't get the same accolades, building a "Hall of Fame" team is desirable. Every teacher and staff member must excel in their roles and be able to contribute to the school as a whole to guarantee that it functions at its highest level. This is where our cycle for branding attracts incredible talent. Building a winning team requires people who want to be a part of the great things being done (Jones, Thomas-EL, & Vari, 2020). This requires an unrelenting dedication to telling your school's story and highlighting the contributions of our best teachers. These efforts generate attention, which leads to attraction. Attracting qualified candidates makes recruiting much easier. Showcasing teachers, especially the very best, builds a team that others will want to be a part of and excel in. They will see purpose, success, and appreciation. People want to be a part of something great, and if your school is doing incredible things for students through incredible classroom experiences, others will want to join. Using your superstars to brand your school will benefit them and help to recruit your next group of awesome people.

Too often, recruitment strategies are passive. A vacancy arises, the job is posted, and we wait to see who applies. In this particular educational climate with a shortage of teachers, these tactics fall short as too late and ineffective. The school that builds a great brand wins. The reputation will outperform a job posting every time. Word of mouth is faster and when it's positive and social proof takes over. With tools as easy as LinkedIn, it's almost irresponsible to not actively recruit for top talent through ambitious branding efforts. Using the S.P.A. treatment for your best teachers will profit your whole system as you attract more people like them.

 ## The Bottom Line

Schooling has changed considerably over the last several decades and what is happening in schools should be showcased for the world to see. Every day in the classroom is not glamorous, nor should it be, but meaningful and engaging classroom learning led by highly effective teachers is what needs to be at the forefront of the school narrative. Effective school branding is about identifying what the school is truly about and then putting it on display in every possible way.

Our best teachers are making strides to our school priorities, and that needs to be the narrative, not what folks typically see on the news. When someone thinks of your school, what do you want them to think? Which emotions and feelings do you want to stir within them? If they were going to describe your school, what words would they use? These questions are at the heart of defining your school brand. The right answers to these questions will honor and recognize teachers, support initiatives, champion students, and continue to attract staff who will only reinforce the brand that you are looking to build.

Using the S.P.A. treatment – stories, priorities, and attraction – demonstrates to the community that our best teachers are doing great work and deserve celebrity status. It shows the community that we're setting goals and working toward our priorities, and you'll attract more people who want to be a part of a winning team. Going beyond business cards, like the use of #NCCVTWorks, is your next step to supporting your best teachers and the way they feel about the school where they work.

HOW TO MAKE YOUR INITIAL DEPOSIT

We said that you needed an army of branders, but you may not even be on Instagram or other social media platforms. It's not as difficult or time-consuming as you might think and it's easy to get going. Your first step if learning a new platform seems daunting is to read your school or district's social media policy. If it allows, get a school Instagram Facebook, or other social media account that your community values, find one person who would like to post to it once a day, and you're investing and making strides in no time. If your policy doesn't allow for this, work to adopt a new policy. Until then, start with photos. Take tons of pictures for your newsletter, which at least reaches your staff and families with the great things that your best teachers are doing and that others can see and replicate.

4

Tailoring Professional Learning

Samantha and the Smartboard

Quality professional learning (PL) is a staple for successful schools. Unfortunately, school leaders sometimes learn that the PL was too general, unaligned, or worse yet, impractical. These are just a few of the words associated with poor professional learning. For PL to be effective and improve teacher capacity a few key elements are needed. Samantha's experience highlights what good PL should look like.

Samantha was ecstatic when she found out she was getting a Smartboard in her classroom. She had seen a Smartboard used effectively in one of her colleague's classrooms but didn't know how to use a Smartboard herself or how to create grade-specific lessons for her own students. This is true of many new instructional technologies. From Smartboards to iPads, some teachers have them and know how to use them. Others have them and don't know how to use them well. And, many teachers still, in 2023, may not have much access to instructional tech, while others have access but may underutilize it.

Samantha was hopeful that she could develop engaging lessons where students learn interactively across all subject areas by using this new device. Because the Smartboard is a lot like an iPad where the items are controlled on the screen by touching them, she knew that it would help her create greater engagement

DOI: 10.4324/9781003321316-4

and interaction with her first-graders. The potential with this device was incredible. She was looking forward to the PL but was also concerned.

The school's last stint at running PL on new instructional technology left a lot to be desired. However, she already felt that this one would be better. The teachers who were participating were all new to this technology and that alone was a big change. Typically, there was no differentiation, which frustrated many of the participants. Also, Samantha received the Smartboard Icon on her computer, which corresponded with the training and what she could access ahead of time. Lastly, she received a list of What To Do and What to Expect in preparation of the PL. All good signs.

As the teachers assembled in the Media Center, the trainers were ready to go, and there were three tech specialists available for teachers who needed assistance. The directions were on the presenters' Smartboard in the main room, and there was excitement to get the workshop started. The structure for this PL was not a one-size-fits-all approach. There were various options from which teachers could choose. The first was How to Effectively Use Your Smartboard and only novices attended. There was another session for those teachers who were competent and proficient with the tool but wanted to learn more from teachers who were using the device in different ways. And, another session for expert users who wanted to know more about the features that they weren't using yet, features that were described in the session description.

As the facilitators got started, all teachers were able to watch demonstrations with ample time to work independently at stations or back in their room with their own boards. The instructor used an I Do, You Do process that worked well for teachers who wanted to practice. Samantha even had time to begin working on creating a lesson plan for her class that showcased her new skills with the instructional technology. At the end of the three-hour PL, Samantha walked away knowing how to set up her device properly, how to use basic but important tools, and best of all, she completed her first lesson plan that would use the device to engage students.

Although Samantha's experience was positive, based on the tiered approach, by skill level, too often school-based PL falls short. Teachers' skills and experiences are so vast that general PL is almost never a good idea. This was true for Samantha, but imagine your best Smartboard user attending the same PL that Samantha experienced, yet that's what we do to our best people all the time. This PL is exactly what the best teachers do on a regular basis – meet the students where they are and help each of them move forward.

The Costs Associated With One-Size-Fits-All Professional Learning

Unfortunately, a generic one-size-fits-all approach to PL is far too common in schools. Nondescript PL that is designed for the masses, while lacking the uniqueness and characteristics that represent the diversity of the instructional staff, is insufficient. The limitations of PL of this kind are evident in the classroom, as staff aren't fully equipped to use the tools and resources that are intended to create dynamic, rigorous, socially, technologically, and culturally responsive classrooms. What's needed is PL that is tailored – a customized learning opportunity that helps create highly skilled professionals equipped to lead their classrooms.

When we search for PL services in education that meet this criteria – ones that represent the individual needs of our teachers – we come up short. Yes, some schools and districts are taking this approach, but it's rare. Rather, we point to PL services that are sometimes offered in the business world to demonstrate how tailoring PL can work to build the capacity of each person as an individual. In all of our research on this topic, Accenture quickly rises to the top. A Fortune Global 500 company, Accenture is a professional services firm led by CEO Julie Sweet. When a company is designed to deliver PL answers in a myriad of industries from aerospace to energy (Accenture, 2020) they have to differentiate to meet the needs of a diverse workforce.

A quick dive into Accenture's business model reveals their passion and focus for professional learning. They tout that "innovation never stops. And neither do we" (Accenture, 2020). As such, they offer learning in three primary modalities:

1. Connected Classrooms
2. Online Courses
3. Learning Boards

The Connected Classrooms allow experts to connect with one another no matter where they physically are located. This promotes learning that is fluid and managed by the learner. Accenture created "learning bots," which are a curated set of information from an expert designed in a way that the learner can engage with the material. The Online Courses are completely focused on developing people by increasing and improving their skill set. Accenture calls this "upskilling," which is directly tied to a person's position and geographical location.

Unfortunately, professional learning in schools often fails to meet this degree of sophistication. The PL suffers from superfluity – trying to cover too much information, from legislated changes to mandated modules. Schools become the nest for instructional and non-instructional PL, working to benefit the whole child or any number of other interests. All of this is necessary, but it also pulls away from what each teacher actually needs, including our best teachers who may benefit from a more tailored approach than backbones and mediocres.

Accenture's model for PL and the degree of tailoring that they provide – taking into account how the needs within the same industry may differ in different parts of the world – maximizes employee development. Their final model, the Learning Board, is described as "offering real-time, right sized learning" from experts. This is a way that school systems can begin to think about PL differently, especially for highly skilled and technical positions.

The power in the Accenture offerings is that all three learning modalities function to create a holistic environment for the organizations they serve. Although learning for teachers may appear to be different within K-12 education, and perhaps lack some of the technological sophistication that a Global 500 company may have, the ability to connect teachers to various modes of professional learning that is differentiated for their needs is powerful – and possible. If the professional learning is designed and tailored to fit teachers' skills and levels of understanding, with an emphasis on the uniqueness of the student population they serve, learning can and will be incredible. What we need is to picture this for our best teachers, whose skills and development are just different from that of our backbone teachers.

Always keep in mind that the personalization and varied approaches sound like the right thing to do in every case, but if the quality isn't there, the variation loses its value. Additionally, many of us have been in at least a few large group PL sessions that we found effective for learning. The value of the PL is more important than anything else. Turning everything into a personalized experience is sort of like saying that we want to see less direct instruction in our classrooms when what we really need is less ineffective direct instruction from teachers who don't do it well. We're sure that you have teachers who use direct instruction and are really good at it. We do not want to lose that gift by forcing everyone to disavow it. Instead, what we're trying to do is to reduce ineffectiveness. That said, your best teachers are the most likely to need a personalized approach, even if it means a large group scenario, but maybe one that isn't the same large group as what the rest of your teachers need. When we say "personalized," we don't necessarily mean one-on-one.

The intent and goals for PL are the same in education as in any other business or company, in that the employee's skills, in our case, educators, must be responsive to the consumer, the students. A culture of individualized PL embraces the fact that teachers should be continually developed to grow as specialized experts. Accenture's ecosystem of learning, across many industries, guarantees that their employees have access to experts on engaging and varied platforms, so learning is continuous. But, most importantly, the Accenture example embraces the need to continually advance an employee's knowledge and skills based on a continuum versus one-size-fits-all.

The reality is that teachers need ongoing, specialized skill development that continues to refine and support their needs;

this includes using various learning modalities within their specialty area as it relates to the diverse population they are educating. Today's school setting demands progressive efforts for greater student achievement. As schools rapidly change in new ways, from the students themselves to the ever-evolving world we are preparing them for, teachers need dynamic tools that they can masterfully use within the classroom. This means that your best teachers may need, or be ready for, a very different program regarding PL than some of the other teachers in your school or district, and it starts with an understanding of where they are on the training and skill development of their domain. That's why your next step is to use the Professional Learning Matrix to evaluate the needs of your best teachers.

Investment #4: Assess Using the Professional Learning Matrix

The approach to tailored and diverse professional learning (PL) begins with how it is perceived by school leaders and what the vision and the goals are of the school. PL is the progressive pursuit of refined knowledge and skill development. The first step along this journey begins with a clear understanding of the methods that are most effective and how they are best employed in the classroom. As Burchard (2017) posits, "clarity is the child of careful thought and mindful experimentation." Educational leaders who take this type of surgical approach to professional learning, carefully decide which strategies are most impactful, and then tailor PL to meet the needs of teachers along a continuum of where they are with the identified strategy. Knowing what works, and where each individual stands with it, holds the power to transform professional learning by abandoning the one-size-fits-all that is the typical approach.

We are fortunate that the research around what works in schools has exploded over the years. From formal and informal writings and from educational researcher to practitioner, there are tremendous resources available that school leaders can lean on to improve their system. It is the second step that proves more challenging and that is how to go about teaching those proven methods, especially as our best teachers hone their skills on their own.

Professional Learning Matrix

Successful teacher development and professional learning (PL) must be anchored in three primary areas. One, PL needs to be explicit. There should be no doubt on what is going to be learned, why it is important, and how it can be used in the classroom to support student achievement. Two, teacher development needs to be intentional. Teachers' skill development and the goals of the school should be aligned. This ensures that the relationship between the goals of the school and the training are working in harmony. Each element of PL should support the goals of the school, while the goals directly drive the PL that is being provided. Third, PL needs to be on a continuum of rigor. It should be robust, diverse, and increasingly more rigorously applied. Rarely do we consider training teachers on a skill and moving them from novice to excellence, but that's what your best teachers want and need.

If those three areas of PL sound familiar it is because those are three components of what the most effective teachers do in their classrooms every day. The goal is to teach the adults in the manner which the best teachers already teach the students. It isn't creating something new, it is transferring the knowledge within our school – that the best teachers have and use – to a broader application, the faculty and staff.

Too often, PL is really training on a program or curriculum or tool. There is nothing inherently wrong with this type of learning, but it should not be confused with PL. Training alone falls short of developing the whole teacher. This makes the learning experience choppy, fragmented, and nonlinear. Having PL on a continuum creates long-term clarity, which is critical for enduring success over time. Regrettably, this is often the most overlooked aspect of superior professional learning. Let's be clear, training teachers on how to use a curriculum or tool is quite different than assessing their needs as a professional and providing PL that is tailored to their specific skill set.

The first two areas, explicitness and intentionality, are more common within school-based PL. This kind of knowledge and understanding is necessary for all teachers to have. That said, standards-based education helped normalize these first two areas, providing guidance through standards and performance targets that help unify curriculum. Our best teachers have a firm handle on this. They understand what to teach so that a greater focus can be on how to teach. It is within the "how" where we can empower all teachers, including our best.

When the "how" is at the center of PL, the focus is on learning. The content, instruction, assessments, and student experience must all be calculated within the equation. This requires schools to look at their professional learning through a multifaceted lens to determine its effectiveness and quality. For example, focusing on a new curriculum and failing to recognize the diversity of learners in a class can prove to be very shortsighted.

The curriculum can be aligned to the standards, fully understood by the teacher, which still falls within the "what" aspect of the formula. When teachers know the curriculum and standards well enough to plan lessons, it's the "how" that's left to figure out. And, we contend that the focus has been so laser-like on the "what" that the "how" is just now receiving the attention that it deserves. Teachers, especially our best, need to be thought about in terms of their skill and development with not just training on what they teach but their expertise with how they teach. This is a critical missing component of teacher development.

Teacher Development

T.J. and Joe first introduced the following Professional Learning Matrix, shown in Figure 4.1, in their book *Candid and Compassionate Feedback* (Jones & Vari, 2019). Originally developed as a method to differentiate leadership development for teacher leaders, its versatility extends to all educators as we look at a growth model within specific domains.

The vertical axis refers to the individual's position, while the horizontal axis refers to the individual's skills. The four quadrants represent areas of growth with topical development being the quadrant designed for a highly skilled person within their specialized area of expertise.

The first quadrant denotes foundational knowledge, which is mostly associated with general training at a novice skill level.

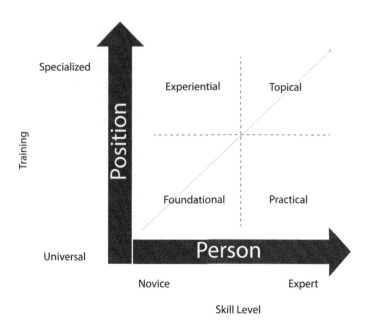

FIGURE 4.1

Often times, PL in schools may be stationed at this primary stage. Here, for example, we're training everyone to use a tool or curriculum that they haven't used before. The second quadrant, practical, advances the skill level of the person within very discreet and developmental ways. This would be a PL that is designed for teachers who know and use a curriculum well enough to become experts. The training is still universal, but the trainer knows that many of the teachers in the room have a foundational knowledge already. We find this to be less rare than the general PL, but still is not the norm.

Too often, the limitation of our PL in schools is that it's too universal in nature – PL that targets basic understanding and leaves those who already have it unchallenged. The third quadrant, experiential, represents the opposite of quadrant two. This training is highly specialized but not necessarily tailored to the individual's needs and profile for growth. Here, we drive the conversation back to the "what" versus the "how." An experiential, specialized training might be about something particular to the curriculum but not "how" to teach the curriculum to a group of less than eager students, for example.

The fourth quadrant, topical, is where we ultimately want our learning to live for our best teachers – our experts in this area. This is the quadrant in which the teacher is operating and learning at an expert level within a highly specialized area. Now, we're finally targeting a skill in a specialized area to an expert degree. Until we reach this final quadrant, our best teachers aren't getting what they need and deserve.

The goal of the matrix is to consciously focus on developing each person within multiple areas. There will be times when foundational learning will be enough and there will be times when we want the person to grow in expertise. One common misuse of this matrix, and others like it, is ranking the quadrants in order of importance. We caution you not to view the quadrants in order of superiority, but rather to provide clear guidance on the level of the professional learning and information on a teacher's skill level. That is, except with your best teachers.

Your best teachers should always be thought of in the specialized, expert, and topical areas of the quadrants to further their development and differentiation from backbones and mediocres. This is not to say that your best teachers won't need foundational training on occasion, but if you only provide them the foundation that you do with others, they'll get frustrated and, worse yet, their potential will stagnate.

School leaders need to use the Skill Development Matrix to assess teacher knowledge and expertise, and this is especially true for our best teachers who will only benefit from PL that is specialized, topical, and designed for their level of expertise. An investment in the use of the matrix to determine what our best teachers need is an investment in what they can do with proper PL when they're back in front of their students.

Maximizing Your Investment: Avoid The Iceberg Effect

The concept of mastery is not new in schools; however, the focus is usually on student work and not on teacher development and growth. Schools are familiar with identifying what exemplary work looks like for students' activities and assignments.

Teachers work to define what mastery looks like so that we know the aim of the lesson, unit, or curriculum map. This level of clarity helps students achieve the target (Chappuis & Stiggins, 2017). Whether we're assessing an essay or a musical performance, educators have conscientiously worked to create clarity around levels of performance that distinguish between novice and exemplary work.

Teachers strive to build learning environments that empower students within the classroom to trust the learning process and to embrace the notion that their own learning and performance is limitless (Bergen, 2013). Some schools and districts are further along on this journey, but our best teachers have thought about mastery since the beginning of the one-room schoolhouse.

No matter, though, these efforts are a work-in-progress that require teachers to be experts in a variety of areas. Teachers must have dynamic interpersonal skills so that they are equipped to create a culture of inclusivity among students and productively collaborate with other teachers. Creating dynamic classrooms that hold students to high standards, engage them, and support them in very deliberate ways requires extensive and intricate training.

Despite this need, many schools fall into a trap that we call The Iceberg Effect, illustrated in Figure 4.2. This is when a new idea, skill, or technology is introduced only at the surface level, but we somehow establish a fallacy that what was presented was also mastered. Ninety percent of an iceberg is below the water

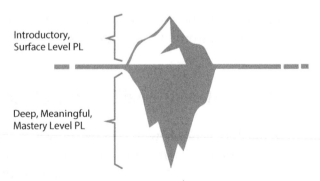

Introductory, Surface Level PL

Deep, Meaningful, Mastery Level PL

FIGURE 4.2

line (United States Geological Survey, n.d.) and like much of our current PL practices, a lot of what should and could be learned lies below the surface and never gets explored, taught, or understood. We end up thinking that people know more about an initiative, program, or practice when they don't have more than an overview of it.

By not taking the adequate time or providing the necessary support to fully develop a teacher's skill, training remains at an introductory level, resulting in teachers not receiving the deep and differentiated PL that is needed to cultivate expertise. Because our best teachers often have these basic skills, we miss the opportunity to delve into the depths of what would equip them with the details and nuances of greatness.

Not getting into the specifics of the learning causes our best teachers to become frustrated. Teachers recognize the limitations of surface level PL and know that it will not positively impact their performance in the classroom. When our PL remains at an introductory stage, the teachers only begin to scratch the surface of their understanding and contemplation about what it looks like in action.

A better approach to PL, and ways to avoid The Iceberg Effect, is by assessing teachers' level of expertise using the Professional Learning Matrix. By using the Matrix, we meet the learning needs of all educators; their learning should be tiered and structured systematically so that novices, experts, and everyone in between gets what they need. This rarely occurs and it hurts our best teachers the most because they're ready to move to deeper depth than others who still may need the surface level learning. The Matrix allows us to evaluate our best teachers' needs to ensure that the PL is either differentiated in the same space with all teachers or actually provides a separate training depending on expertise.

The reality is that the skill levels of your teachers may be quite varied. But that's not an excuse to provide one-size-fits-all PL, and your best teachers are always the ones that suffer the most from it. Use the Matrix and apply The Iceberg Effect to make better PL decisions for your superstars, and everyone will win in the end.

👥 How the Professional Learning Matrix Profits the Whole System

Starting with our best teachers, using the Professional Learning Matrix when we build PL experiences is no different than analyzing students' needs and determining the best course of action regarding teaching and learning. Once we develop experts in our school, we then have highly successful working models that can build confidence in newer or less sophisticated learners. When we're building students' schedules or creating lesson plans, the awareness of the diversity of learning needs is reflected in the planning. When we get the schedule right or a lesson plan nailed for our students, all students benefit. This is how the Matrix serves the school. It helps inform those designing PL to fully grasp the diversity of skill among the teaching core. When we differentiate for our teachers the learning is more meaningful and more practical. Moreover, our best teachers' PL needs will be met, and all teachers will get what they deserve.

The Matrix is also designed to measure any new employees during the onboarding process and throughout the first few months. School personnel are forever changing, and schools are looking to fill positions more now than ever, particularly in high need areas. This new reality within education complicates offering meaningful PL. The use of the Matrix creates the opportunity for school leaders to determine precisely not only where their existing staff members' skills lie, but also anyone they hire. In the long run this saves an enormous amount of time when leveling up new hires or discovering that some new hires may already possess the fundamental skills you are looking for in a teacher.

The goal is to always hire the best candidate with the greatest skill set. Why not inventory and determine their skill set, rather than misuse their time on learning that they may already know? And, if your school is attracting exemplary teachers, then identifying PL that will make them grow will help the school reach its goals that much sooner. Great schools recognize the need to meet teachers where they are not only for the individual's development but to aggressively and thoughtfully ensure high levels of student achievement.

The Bottom Line

Despite its attempt at efficiency, one size rarely fits all. This holds true for apparel and professional learning (PL). General and introductory PL is indispensable because the foundational aspects from which all enduring learning comes are critical for everyone as we progress from novice to expert. Whether it is effectively developing an individual education program (IEP) for a student or learning how to use online formative assessments as teachers, the foundational training and learning should come first.

But, when some teachers have the foundational knowledge, acquired through PL or on their own, their needs must be assessed to ensure that the subsequent PL is going deep enough to produce growth and development. Otherwise, we continue to frustrate our best teachers with the same old approach to one-size-fits-all models.

This effort only becomes a reality when school leaders grasp that PL needs to be viewed in a dynamic, ongoing continuum that is malleable enough to meet the needs of all teachers. And, thinking about our best teachers first provides us with the insight to differentiate for their skills and move backwards on the continuum for others. The further up on the Matrix that we find our best teachers, the deeper we ought to think about their needs in terms of The Iceberg Effect. This is the power of Accenture – continually offering learning that is innovative, forward thinking, and responsive to the ever-changing world that we live in. Schools can benefit from Accenture's approach as long as they are willing to see the skills of their people, their best people in particular, on a continuum of growth and development.

HOW TO MAKE YOUR INITIAL DEPOSIT

The first step to supporting teachers, especially your best teachers, with a differentiated approach to professional learning is to implement a simple survey. Any leader at any level can do this with ease and the power that it will yield is immense.

Create a spreadsheet with all of your teachers in the left column, and answer two questions in the next two columns: What is one goal for professional learning that you have for each person? and What is one learning goal, from the simple survey of only a few questions, that they have for themselves? With this information in hand, you can start to tailor professional learning with far more ease.

5

Looking Outside School Walls

Professional Learning – For Us, By Us

"Lifelong learning" is a common phrase used within education. Teacher development takes a couple of different paths, from continuing education to earning advanced degrees to professional learning offered or supported within the school system. One thing we know for sure is that our best teachers – and all teachers – need different and unique experiences as learners so that they can continually expand and refine their expertise. The truth of the matter, though, is that the system – including credits earned at local or virtual colleges and universities – is often not equipped to help our most skillful educators. That's when we look for opportunities, even programs, in sometimes faraway places.

We predict that the word "program" might have caught your eye. There is a negative stigma connected to this word. For many, the connotation suggests a rigid, restricted, or canned sequence of steps that stifles innovation and personalization. However, the dictionary definition is "a plan or system under which action may be taken toward a goal." In this chapter, we resurrect the value of embracing experiences that other entities like universities and cohort groups establish to offer exemplary programs. Your best teachers can profit from the comradery gained by learning with other superstars and the expertise the program provides.

DOI: 10.4324/9781003321316-5

Monica, a veteran biology teacher, has participated in such a program – outside of what her school, district, and local higher education agencies can offer – for six years. She is as fired up as she was when she first started teaching all because of her professional learning experiences in this useful, unique, and challenging program. The bottom line for Monica is that it's not just about acquiring new skills and knowledge, but it's also about having a creative outlet to learn and grow among other professionals, in both higher education and the public sector. She expressed that the power of the experience rests with the connections among the participants.

The program we're referring to, and we know that they don't like the word "program," is called the Delaware Teachers Institute (DTI). It is a unique partnership with local school districts in New Castle County Delaware and the College of Arts and Sciences at the University of Delaware. But, it's not just another graduate school program. The goal of DTI is simple: strengthen teaching and learning in Delaware public schools. Although the goal is straightforward, the program should not be mistaken for easy.

As an incredible teacher with many strengths that range from pedagogy to classroom climate, Monica shared that one primary benefit of the program lies in the Yoda level content expertise that the university offers to the participating K-12 classroom teachers. What she really enjoys parallels the unique philosophy of Daymond John, Shark Tank investor and founder of the hip hop apparel company, For Us, By Us, more popularly known as FUBU. The focus of DTI is teacher-centric and embraces the FUBU mentality with a goal of improving teachers' content expertise and curriculum unit development. And, the whole premise is that it's for teachers, by teachers.

Mirrored from a parent program at Yale, the Yale National Initiative, the emphasis is on a concentrated area that encompasses teacher professional growth and creates a very discreet and narrow focus for diving deep into subject matter that includes how to translate that knowledge to effective instructional delivery for students. Monica is privy to various seminars, such as glass blowing and disaster response command centers, that guide her learning and aid in the construction of a teaching unit that she will ultimately use in her biology class. Because the participants undergo a rigorous admission process, their commitment is high and so is their expertise. The degree of professionalism and sophistication of the seminars creates an opportunity for teacher participants to take their teaching to another level. The collegiality among the various entrants, regardless of grade level, content area, or standards taught, is superb.

Monica is a veteran of DTI and is now focusing on biodiversity and working within the Amazon Rainforest Seminar as her first choice for her current focus. She relayed that this in-depth understanding of the Amazon will strengthen her knowledge of biodiversity, allowing her to relate it to many aspects within her curriculum. At the end of the seminar, she'll have a fully developed unit of study that she will use to teach one or more aspects of biology to students in the public school where she works.

The in-depth content knowledge expertise comes from a faculty professor who joins the seminar as a leader; the program is clear that the hierarchy of professor and student is purposefully absent. Everyone brings expertise to the table, and the professors often learn as much about teaching as the teachers learn about content. This is the intersection of expertise and the impending unit will not only have the richness of content, but will also be tailored and curated in a way that will end up being perfectly designed to meet the needs of Monica's students.

The DTI program, like others we'll feature in this chapter, is very specialized and intensive. It recognizes the teacher as an expert, as someone who is continually refining their trade, and it propels teachers to new heights in ways that district-led and general university degrees aren't capable of doing.

The Cost Associated With Limited Opportunities

Umami – a word that is largely unknown outside the culinary world or by cooking enthusiasts. It is one of the five basic tastes, but is not so well known among most people. The translation of the Japanese word is "pleasant savory taste." Despite it not being as identifiable as the other four tastes – sweet, bitter, salty, and sour – umami, albeit subtle, is recognized by our taste receptors. Although people can sense it, the taste is more difficult to describe, more elusive to capture. It's often described as the "meaty, savory deliciousness that deepens flavor" (Anjinomoto, 2022). Umami gives complexity to our foods that make our meals rich and flavorful. Steak, salmon, broth, aged cheeses, chocolate, and green tea are just a few examples of where umami is evident.

You may be wondering why we're describing umami in a book chapter about professional learning (PL), but, just like umami's properties as a satisfactory and complex taste, PL has its own levels of sophistication, uniqueness, and complexity, especially as we translate PL for the needs of an already highly-skilled teacher. When we think about defining PL, we turn to the Learning Policy Institute, which identifies key elements of effective PL, including "discipline-specific curriculum development and pedagogies," "active learning strategies," "sustained duration," "coaching and expert support" (Darling-Hammond, Hyler, & Gardner, 2017). These necessary aspects of PL are clear and understandable but incredibly difficult to achieve. As a master chef works to bring about the power of an ingredient's umami, so should school leaders as we think about the development of PL experiences for our best teachers.

Unfortunately, this isn't what we find. For a myriad of legitimate reasons, school leaders, like classroom teachers, end up designing PL experiences that mostly teach to the middle. Even most conferences, which can be inspiring and informative, don't meet the criteria we describe in this chapter. The reasons are abundant, but let's take a look at two approaches that we see regularly and why they're not productive responses to a school or district's needs.

First, many school leaders will use standardized test scores as the basis for PL decision-making. Interestingly, although this approach might uncover what students need, it doesn't address what the teachers need. We understand why this seems logical, but let's look at a common scenario and why it's not likely to pan out.

Imagine Coolidge Elementary school receives its fifth-grade reading scores from the state assessment only to reveal that the students are underperforming. Worse yet, the latest round of scores demonstrates an even greater drop in overall performance than years past. Coolidge's administration is perplexed. Their teachers are clearly working hard, and they've been using programs that are meant to boost student outcomes. Conclusions are drawn that since the resources and methods for tier one instruction are research-based, there must be a need for further tier two interventions. The actions narrow down to buying an additional program or sending a team to another conference with "intervention" in its title.

We're certainly not against new tools, curriculum updates, or targeted inventions, all of which require training. But, like we outlined with our Professional Learning Matrix, training and PL are not the same. The biggest problem with this approach, though, is that it stems from the mentality that everyone needs the same strategy. The better approach is to look for bright spots and then scale what's working or to make an investment in your best teachers to expand their knowledge and expertise amongst the rest of the staff in ways that we outline throughout this book.

Second, we see school leaders reacting to their need for improvement with an over-reliance on "best practices" and pedagogical trends. This can range from registering teachers to attend a high quality conference event, activating PLCs, or even implementing the use of an identified highly effective instructional strategy. Again, there is nothing inherently wrong with any of this – in fact, we suggest you do all three of these in particular if you haven't already – but these strategies are not enough to meet the needs of your best teachers.

Both approaches are reactive and overlook the skills and needs of teachers. These general improvements might be good ideas, but they don't address any substantial teacher development, especially not in a way that might resonate with your superstars.

This perpetual reactionary response in which schools find themselves will inadvertently limit the growth of their best teachers. In Chapter 4, we covered the depth of professional learning needs for our best teachers. In this chapter, we empha-size the diversity and uniqueness of specialized programming that will meet their needs now that you know what their needs are. When using the Professional Learning Matrix, you're getting to know what your best teachers truly need if they're going to get better; here, we're demonstrating just how far you might have to go to get them what you identified.

For our best teachers to get what they need, their PL might need to go beyond the school walls. Think about a master chef and how ridiculous it would be for a manager to give him a new knife and expect the food to taste better. Of course, a better knife might make minor improvements, and a cook with a dull knife can work safer and faster with a sharper one. But, your best teachers are mixing up the umami using a dull knife. Chefs, the best in the world, don't typically learn their skills in a restaurant around the corner. They go as far as needed to find specialized programs to get expert experiences from the best in the world. That's what your superstar teachers need when we think about and plan their growth.

Investment #5: Get S.E.T. for Success

In his best-selling book, *The World is Flat*, Thomas Friedman introduced us to the amazing concept that the modern world is actually flat. Not physically of course, but in an age of globaliza-tion and new technologies, it has never been easier to connect from person to person, business to business, or from country to country (Friedman, 2005). Friedman's theory, which was ground-breaking when it was first introduced in 2005, is even more applicable today. The rise and use of the internet make access to information, tools, resources, and other educators almost effort-less at this point. It also makes finding specialized programs for teacher development easier than ever before.

Typically, when we think of the implications of a flat world in our schools, we think about how we can design learning expe-riences for our students that will prepare them for this ever-changing world. In fact, if you want to have fun, take a quick look at many school and district vision statements and you will most likely find words and phrases like, "competitive global society," "world-class," or even "preparing students for the 21st Century." The visions are written to be progressive, while acknowledging that the knowledge and skills we teach within our schools must prepare students for a future we may not yet even grasp ourselves.

While it's important to prepare our students for this global flat world that has come to be, schools must also ask themselves, "how well are we equipping our teachers to meet this demand?" It's through our teacher's growth and learning that our students will learn the fundamental skills, such as critical thinking and idea origination. Now that we've accepted that the world is flat, so many years after Friedman's work was first published, schools have embraced global networks, web-based advantages, and new resources for students. But, have we done the same for teachers?

Think back to Chapter 3 where we talked about branding your school on social media. You know a quick way to learn how to do that? Follow schools that are already doing a good job with social media and do what they do. All you are really doing is drawing from their best. Think about how quickly those in your school can replicate when they don't have to innovate. This is exactly what the best teachers do on social media. Your outstanding fifth-grade teachers look connected with other great fifth-grade teachers anywhere in the world. The same thing is true with your chemistry teacher, your eighth-grade math teacher, etc. This allows the knowledge of one to become the knowledge of all. It is exactly what you want to do within your schools but you have quick (and free) access to others anywhere. By doing this we quickly learn to grow. If the world is flat for sure we don't want to fall off.

We want our focus to remain on the proven PL models that provide essential frameworks for learning through continual refinement of teaching practices. By optimizing PL through the lens of our best teachers' skill enhancement, school leaders can leverage the power of extended learning opportunities (ELOs). These opportunities are for those teachers who have mastered

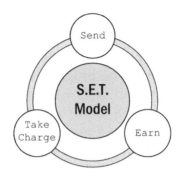

FIGURE 5.1

the fundamental elements of teaching and learning and require a different level of training or PL to become better at their craft.

As we unpack the essence of an ELO, we do so using our S.E.T. Model, illustrated in Figure 5.1, to demonstrate both the power in what can be provided to your best teachers as well as a model that enhances everyone else. We'll describe S.E.T. as the foundation and we embed examples of the types of ELOs that are emerging around the country as places where our best teachers can truly get what they deserve.

Because not all school systems have the expertise within their own walls, we start with the need to send our best teachers out so that they return better than when they left. This isn't a knock on a school's or district's ability to grow their people at all, but rather the realization that we must take advantage of ELOs that are available beyond our school walls. It may also be a way to speed up the growth process.

Send – Send Your Best Teachers to the Far Reaches of the Earth

As teachers' skills become more advanced, the same goes for the kind of PL they need. This is where unique learning opportunities emerge as the necessary next step. These are teachers that have strong foundational and conceptual understanding of their content and the pedagogy required to deliver it to students; as such, their PL must be different.

The problem with just recognizing that their PL must be different is that we don't always offer different on our own soil. That's why the first aspect of S.E.T. is Send. At the point in which we realize that our best teachers need someone else to help them grow, we can either find them a Yoda (as we've discussed so far), or we can send them out to a specialized ELO. That's where they'll develop a new skill, deepen their understanding of the content or pedagogy, and return with a refreshed reality about teaching that can benefit all of us and our students.

Earn – Allow Your Best Teachers to Earn Status Through Unique Certificates, Credentials, and Credits

Before we dive into what this professional learning looks like, we want to draw a clear line of distinction between extended learning opportunities (ELOs) and continuing education credits. Teacher compensation packages are often tied to continuous schooling. States nearly guarantee teachers will participate in on-going learning by requiring academic credits or some form of continuing education units. To the benefit of some teachers in various districts, there is a financial reward for racking up credits through accredited universities or pre-approved professional learning events.

There are benefits to a system that ensures continuous learning in this way. Graduate courses and isolated learning events check off requirements to renew teacher certifications and move teachers' salaries up the pay scale. Conversely, ELOs aren't only about going back to school or attending conferences or signing up for seminars. Rather, they are very refined areas of focus that are supported by elite programming and unique opportunities.

As a bonus to involve your best teachers in ELOs, they do offer credits in some cases, in other cases they offer credentials or certificates; in any case, they provide a dignified status for participating teachers and the school systems where they work. We detail a few in the next section that we are familiar with and that epitomize quality PL in a flat world with very strategic and differentiated components. Our goal for sharing these offerings is so that you have an idea of what quality ELOs offer. Your job is to find others of similar quality for your teachers.

The first ELO that we want to highlight is the University of Pennsylvania's Graduate School of Education Center for Professional Learning, which is built specifically for educators.

For example, they have a Project-Based Learning program, which their site describes as follows: "The Project-Based Learning certificate program is designed for current educators who strive to create rich, meaningful, and rigorous learning experiences through student-centered approaches to teaching and learning" (University of Pennsylvania GSE, 2022). This program is a yearlong, intensive, very acute offering with expert coaches that elevate teachers' status by working with them throughout the year. This certificate-based program also has a diverse and highly skilled instructional team. The professors come from acclaimed universities like Johns Hopkins and Harvard, as well as practitioners who are still working within the school system. Even though this is a UPenn program, the mentors are from various diverse settings.

Another unique offering is Harvard's Data Wise program. Unlike the PBL certificate course that runs over the course of a year, Data Wise is five very intense days (Harvard GSE, n.d.). One thing that we find extremely beneficial is that this PL requires a team, which should be composed of a school leader, a teacher, and another educator in a leadership role, such as school counselor. Schools are inundated with data but not the tools and resources for how to use the data.

Data holds the key to unlock many insights for how to improve a school, but too often it's underused or worse, misused. Data availability doesn't mean educators are skilled at using it effectively. Schools don't have time to go down costly and lengthy roads that yield little results because administrative teams and teachers misinterpreted or used the wrong data for a decision. Data Wise solves that problem, and imagine putting your best teachers in the driver's seat with this kind of status, which they certainly can't get from their school or district.

Both opportunities offer very refined PL, again with mentoring embedded. Not only are they effective ELOs, but they offer some of the best minds for educators to work with throughout the program. There are other unique offerings as well. The University of Delaware offers the Delaware Teachers Institute (DTI) (featured in the story that begins this chapter), which has a competitive application process for local teachers. This seminar-based program is led by highly skilled university faculty members who work with exceptional K12 teachers, which culminates with the teacher creating a curriculum unit that is published for open-source use by other teachers. Something else noteworthy about DTI is that it is a part of a national network of local teacher institutes that started at Yale. This, too, is something that your best teachers will not only enjoy, but it elevates them to the status that they deserve.

The last program that we want to highlight is the Galileo Institute for Teacher Leadership. It's regarded as an elite country club; members join by invitation only, which are offered to the superstars of schools throughout the Detroit area. Cohorts learn together over two years under the program's premise that we need to rely on our teachers if we want to have sustainable growth in our schools. Bob Maxfield founded the institute to amplify the voices of teachers and give them the opportunity to become leaders equipped with specific leadership skills and teaching expertise. Some Galileo leaders naturally find their way to principal positions. However, the program is not grooming them to be future administrators. The goal, rather, is to strengthen teacher leaders (Oakland University, 2021).

One way that the Galileo veterans serve the program with their established leadership skills is to remain as alumni and advisers for future cohorts. Upon successful completion of the Galileo Institute for Teacher Leadership, the graduates provide recommendations for future candidates to participate in the next cohort of teacher leaders. This program is about redefining the profession and not only developing great teachers but empowering them. While this model is exclusive to superstar teachers working in Detroit suburbs, schools around the country can adopt a similar model in their areas, starting on a micro-level, to empower their best teachers and give them a voice.

These examples of how schools who are in close geographical areas with each other have developed programs that bring educators together. If you're unaware of these types of opportunities in your region, ask around. Connect at principals' meetings or your state division of national organizations like NAESP and NASSP and inquire about programs available to high quality teachers. It might be a cohort that connects a few times a year or a meeting held for teacher leaders.

Another option available to early childhood, elementary, middle, or secondary teachers in the United States is a certification process through the National Board for Professional Teaching Standards. To become a National Board Certified Teacher (NBCT), teachers focus on four components of teaching. They have access to professional development, coaches, and other NBCT teacher networks as they learn and apply each of the components. Candidates use a blend of constructed responses, work samples, videos, and portfolio evidence to earn this prestigious certification. According to the nbpts.org website, a national survey of effective teachers identified the NBCT process as among the top three most impactful experiences on their professional growth. One teacher said, "…it wasn't just a certification, it was the most impactful professional development I have ever taken on, and my students still benefit to this day."

Each of these programs exposes your superstars to other schools' best teachers. By looking outside your school walls, you surround them with excellence so they build the capacity to take charge when they return to school.

Take Charge – Elevate Your Best Teachers' Status With Programs That Empower Them to Take Charge When They Return Home

All four samples are different in various ways. From the length of the program, the purpose the program serves, or the focus it has, they all have one thing in common: they empower and develop teachers at an advanced level. These types of PL experiences are a real investment in teachers.

The power of programs such as these is that the experience for attendees will positively impact students, and the return-on-investment goes beyond that because they bring new experiences and perspectives to their classrooms, their teams, and the whole school community.

This brings us to our final aspect of our S.E.T. Model. The investment in your best teachers isn't to simply send them to elite programs to earn certificates that get put in a file or hang on a wall. Fueled with unique experiences, valuable connections, and specialized programming, the teachers need to take charge and put their newly acquired knowledge to action. Leaders must entrust these teachers and provide autonomy for them to determine ways to scale their learning.

Each teacher leader will take charge differently. It might mean they tinker with methods in their own classroom before making recommendations for widespread change. In other cases, the learning they earn will provide validation and build their confidence to offer innovative solutions to perpetual problems. It is also possible they will take charge in more subtle ways by sharing current research, proven instructional methods, quality curriculum resources, or helpful methods for using data using what they learned in their ELOs. The point is that formal and informal ways to take charge require trust and autonomy, and it's the leader's job to set that up. We hope you note the irony.

Maximizing Your Investment: Retain Talented Teachers

Education today finds itself in a challenging position due to the lack of individuals entering the workforce. "In 2006, the number of newly licensed teachers made up 22 percent of total college graduates, compared to 2020, when they made up 11 percent of college graduates" (Peetz, 2022). The data is staggering and education will soon be facing a severe teacher shortage if certain realities within the profession do not change.

The teacher shortage issue is complex and varies from state to state, county to county, district to district, and even subject area to subject area. We know that compensation, other attractive industries, and challenges within education all contribute to the growing problem. This puts an enormous amount of pressure on schools to recruit and retain excellent teachers within a limited applicant pool. While efforts to increase the teacher pipeline rests on the shoulders of many, school leaders must work diligently to ensure they keep the teachers they do have in their schools. The last thing a school can afford is to recruit an excellent teacher only to have them leave in search of greener pastures.

The factors contributing to teachers leaving a particular school may be nuanced, but we know that working conditions are often high on the list of why teachers are dissatisfied. There are other factors that may be out of the school's control, such as compensation packages and other benefits, but school conditions can be greatly determined by quality of leadership. Many times people quit their job because they've quit their leader. The S.E.T. Model is designed to treat your best teachers to different and meaningful learning experiences. The ELOs not only improve their skill levels through advanced learning opportunities, but also create another dimension of collaboration and engagement with like professionals beyond the school walls.

One major challenge for educators is isolation for both novice and veteran staff. Schools often work to solve this issue through PLCs and other types of group activities. However, as previously noted, the learning experience has to be suitable for the person, and socialization efforts are nice but sometimes fall short. The opening story of Monica highlights how ELOs add the necessary dimension of sophistication, learning, and camaraderie. Participating teachers feel like professionals because they are treated like one. If there is an accurate over-generalization about teachers, it is that they love to learn. One powerful way to retain teachers is by feeding them dynamic learning opportunities.

Your very best teachers will recognize and appreciate the investment you make in them and, in turn, will not only deliver in the classroom, but will desire to remain a part of an organization that recognizes and supports talent. Additionally, the clout and expertise they gain give them the opportunity to have an active voice in what the school and other teachers may need. This empowerment is vital. We know that trust and respect are two very powerful drives for teacher retainment and by providing them with ELOs create those conditions. Not only do these investments lift individuals, they create unique opportunities to lift the whole system.

How S.E.T. Profits the Whole System

Schools are continually confronting a myriad of challenges and situations that require staff to possess unique and diverse skills within and beyond the classroom walls. The advanced professional learning (PL) that teachers need may not be within their content area yet still may be critical to help students succeed. Consider the emergence of diversity and equity positions or social and emotional learning coordinators in schools. The need for the positions is obvious to school leaders, but the skill set needed by the teachers who are taking these jobs may be lacking. This is where S.E.T. is powerful and lifts the whole system. It allows you to find a unique PL experience that matches the needs of the school and the person who is filling a new role.

Schools across the country have identified equity and inclusion staff, both full time and part time, often at the district and school level. But, a daunting question must be answered: how are these individuals qualified for these roles and which programs have they attended to raise their status at "certified"? Just putting them into the job, even if they are passionate about the work, is often a recipe for failure.

Identifying the skills needed among those who are willing to do the work, finding outside opportunities that are available, and elevating their skills and status is a much better approach. When you put your best teachers in new positions where the goal is that they lift the whole system, it's important to use S.E.T. to set them up for success.

The Bottom Line

Quality teachers with vast experience and well-developed skills emerge as the experts in schools. It's unfortunate that their professional learning (PL) may be stifled due a lack of learning opportunities available to them. Still, continuous PL is necessary for educators to stay on top of their game and abreast of the latest research about teaching and learning. Some PL options have a checkbox feel about them; educators participate in them because they're required. Other opportunities are sometimes misaligned or reactive and fall short of providing what teachers need. When schools limit their options to in-house professional learning, graduate courses chosen in isolation by each teacher, or conferences that offer predetermined, one-and-done exposure to theories and ideas, the power of deep learning and application is deflated. The S.E.T. Model suggests that leaders should send their best teachers to engage in highly specialized programs that provide a level of learning that exceeds what is available anywhere else.

One thing that we mentioned before that is worth saying again is that you should consider sending more than one teacher at a time to these extended learning opportunities (ELOs). The goal is not to isolate your best teachers but rather to elevate them and the rest of the school. Sometimes, sending a few solid backbone teachers with your best teacher to experience these great offerings is exactly the PL need of both your best teachers, because of what the ELO provides, and your backbones, because they're spending time learning with one or more of your best teachers.

We know that these specialty programs can come at a cost, and we also know that many districts frown upon travel. While we understand the limits of budgets, we believe that not allowing travel, even for your best teachers, is a very unfortunate outcome – one that will have an impact on how fast and deep your people can grow and, sometimes, whether or not you retain them. Lastly, when budgets aren't adequate, we suggest seeking grant opportunities or asking outside organizations to help see the vision and fund your best teachers' status upgrade with an ELO that will leave everyone with the satisfactory taste in their mouth only paralleled by the sophistication of umami.

HOW TO MAKE YOUR INITIAL DEPOSIT

This is the one strategy in the book that requires a budget of some sort so we're going to give you three options for your initial investment. 1. If you don't have a budget to send your teachers away for professional learning, do all you can to find money. Look for a grant, a business, or an organization that can provide a stipend that would support teacher professional learning. 2. If you do have a budget and it's small, look for an online course that will excite and meet the needs of a selected teacher. Our friend Mitch Weathers has an online course about executive functioning skills in the classroom that's only $97 dollars (at the time we wrote this book). Courses like this one are available. 3. If you do have a budget and it's large, find the most esoteric far-reaching experience you can and send more than one teacher (at least one "best teacher") to experience it. Remember, you're just getting started, and one of these steps will get you on the path today.

6

Learning and Growing Through Peer Observations

Jeff and the Observation Deck

Expertise varies. People, even within the same profession, possess very different skill sets, some natural and refined over time, others skillfully developed in the field. The avenues to reach these levels of peak performance are as diverse as the individuals themselves. One predominant way to grow at work is through a system that creates opportunities for people to level up. By offering a variety of ways to improve – from job-specific training and coursework to observing peer experts – people can learn very discreet skills. The medical field is one example that exemplifies observational learning as a primary method of teaching new skills. But typically, when we imagine medical students as learners, we think of hospital rounds, and there are so many other versions of a true reflection and implementation model. And, so many more instances where people need to acquire expertise.

Jeff is an accomplished physical therapist (PT) who conducts a very specific type of evaluation within his practice. The evaluation of the patient is nuanced and designed to collect extensive data to determine the patient's true loss of strength. The tests are challenging because of how the patient's body reacts and responds. The daunting question that Jeff must answer is about the extent of the patient's injuries. He must perform a needling

DOI: 10.4324/9781003321316-6

assessment to determine the viability of the patient's claim. Jeff has created a system for other PTs to watch and study him in an effort to train those who are interested in pursuing his specific niche. The ability to use this technique can only be passed on through observation and reflection.

After years of practice, Jeff has learned to trust the data that he gathers through his analysis, including "his eyes." He admits that his own subjective lens must be supported by hard data; but through his experience, his instincts have sharpened. It's this level of expert evaluation that he wants to transfer to his colleagues – seasoned physical therapists who are looking to develop their skills within this specific area of care and evaluation. They aren't rookies, but they want to hone their practice.

Through this working partnership, one aspect of particular importance is the shadowing experience. Shadowing provides a specific time where the other PT observes Jeff to understand the practical implications of the theory as well as the concepts associated with proper application. This process not only trains the observer, it also allows Jeff to continually refine his own skills. Eventually he will work extensively with his newly trained colleagues, breaking down the evaluation to complete all of the critical paperwork. His ability to teach the art and science of the approach simultaneously strengthens his own skills as well.

Jeff was evaluating the patient, running tests, keenly observing, and watching for signs associated with genuine strength loss. One area they pay special attention to is the effort that the patient is exerting during the evaluation. He has to ask himself: Is the patient demonstrating "good effort" during these exercises? The observation is thorough, descriptive, and intense. Jeff looks for "red flags," "aberrant" results. As the load increases, he should see the patient's mechanics begin to falter. With this exercise, the deadlift in this case, the patient extended her knees before her hips and the trainee recognized the change.

This was a pivotal moment in the relationship between the trainer and the apprentice, where the learner actually cued Jeff, demonstrating a transfer of skills. After the evaluation was complete, the trainee asked a very specific question about the movement pattern, which required Jeff to further explain the details of his observation and analysis. This process is a powerful way for the up-and-coming PT to become independent, but it also reinforces and even improves upon Jeff's expertise as he explains the intricacies and nuances of his experienced approach to this very specialized patient assessment.

The Costs Associated With Show-and-Tell Models

In an effort to spread greatness within our schools, it's common practice for our best teachers to be invited to share their successes and skills with the rest of the staff in forums such as PLCs, faculty meetings, and professional learning sessions. In a nutshell, we assign them to the role of professional development presenter because we want them to demonstrate their expertise to the rest of the staff. Unfortunately, this type of professional learning can showcase the great work that our superstars are doing but serve more as a show-and-tell and does not necessarily create the level of change that we want in the other classrooms. The goal is to leverage the expertise within our schools and honor the work and achievements from our most effective instructors, but it doesn't always translate that way to the rest of the faculty.

It seems perfectly logical for school leaders to hand over the staff meeting microphone to their best teachers so listeners will take interest in making improvements in their own classrooms, based on what they hear from their co-worker. The assumption is that this interest, often occurring as a time constrained summary, will somehow transfer into a more universal knowledge of how to replicate the accomplishments being described for school-wide implementation. A lot of the information we know about how people learn best contradicts this model, which is, unfortunately, common in many schools. This does not mean there is never value in this approach; however, there may be ways to reduce the glare of the narrow spotlight that this method places on your best teachers while also increasing their positive impact. Leaders who know their schools well can weigh the credibility and acceptance of their "teacher trainers" at the same time as balancing any risk of them being seen as more of an outsider than a peer.

While this may be appropriate in certain situations and settings – providing time for the best teachers in your school to describe what they do so that everyone else will follow suit – we suggest using a different approach. The first reason is that a *sharing* format is not the same as a *teaching* format. When the goal is to expand practices that are successful in one or more classrooms, your staff will likely learn better in a professional learning format than they will because of a "show-and-tell" time.

In other words, if you want teachers to pick up key strategies from their peers, make sure that you dedicate enough time for your best teachers to introduce an idea or concept apart from just sharing what they do. The topic itself then becomes the focus, such as phonemic awareness or teaching bell-to-bell and less about what Mrs. Best Teacher is doing in her classroom. Additionally, if a share out is not given proper attention and sufficient time, it positions the audience as listeners. Listening is a passive activity, and, just like in the classroom, it's better to engage them in thinking, applying, and connecting to make their new learning stick.

The second reason is that learning new concepts is best reinforced through an emotional connection brought on by an experience (Medina, 2015). In this case, the teachers receiving the professional learning (PL) are less connected emotionally unless the presenter authentically engages the audience and puts on a show for their peers.

And the third reason is that a summary description of a best practice may lead to confirmation bias. The masses simply have thoughts like "yup, I do that, too" or "don't we all do that in our classroom?" The reality is that the purpose of school leaders using master teachers to instruct other staff members is to influence precision – using the best teachers as an example is typically not about introducing something new but rather a more precise way to teach using a certain strategy that needs to be perfected. This is almost impossible to do without seeing it in practice and discussing the nuances.

This is a reminder that the environment and structure of professional learning is important. Some PL lends itself nicely to a room of adults who can gain new knowledge through discussion, demonstration, reading, or even role play. However, some things are difficult to explain or recreate without an actual classroom. For example, a PL setting will likely meet the needs for a workshop on creating alternate and authentic assessments. However, if the topic is maximizing instructional time through smooth transitions and the use of routines, ten minutes in a classroom that has this down pat will be far more powerful than ten minutes in a staff meeting. The setting is critical. There's something about seeing it live and in action that, in our experience, motivates the observers to want to replicate what they see students in other classrooms are capable of doing.

When you identify a skill or method that one of your teachers is the best at – remember this could be one of your backbones who has a special knack for how they lead a restorative circle but might not be a superstar just yet – be mindful of the restrictions caused by offering a PL experience outside a purely natural setting. Take a look at Figure 6.1 in terms of how the roles that the teacher holds are altered when they are asked to present their classroom accomplishments to other educators without the comfort of their classroom and their students.

In addition to the artificial atmosphere of teaching adult peers in the PL room, the new environment impacts your best teacher in the way she is thinking about instruction. Asking dynamic teachers to share their successes with other teachers eliminates

Teacher's Role in the Classroom	Teacher's Role in the Professional Learning
Teacher is teaching students	Teacher is teaching adults
Classroom culture is developed by teacher	School culture is developed by leadership
Teacher is implementing strategy or initiative	Teacher is describing or recreating strategy or initiative
Teacher uses daily	Teacher delivers once in isolation
Part of everyday teacher duties	Beyond regular teacher duties

FIGURE 6.1

the organic flow of teaching and learning that happens between students and teachers in the classroom. The comfort level of teaching students is not always matched when faced with a room full of peers. Many teachers, even our best ones, may get nervous when presenting to adults. Obviously there is no guarantee that simply because a teacher has ease and flow in her classroom that the feeling of that learning space will automatically transfer to a professional learning setting. The magic that can be observed between a teacher and her students is replaced with a description or artificial replication of that magic at best. At its worst, there is a chance it creates a divide between the listeners and who the leader is touting as the model, which can easily set the stage for skepticism from the mediocres and backbones.

The reasons why this doesn't work well are plenty, but the primary problem is that at times teaching and learning with adults may be far different than observing it unfold with students. Imagine if Jeff, the physical therapist referenced at the beginning of the chapter, simply described the exercises and the patient's responses to them. His mentee's transfer of knowledge would have been heavily guided by what Jeff chose to share and how he shared it. However, because Jeff was able to expose his trainee to the experience, the opportunity to notice details critical to the success of the therapy session provided a much higher level of inclusion. When leaders observe greatness in practice, they want the teacher to describe what they observed for the rest of the faculty. The description itself, even if it's modeled, only goes so far as replicable.

One possible flaw is that this type of expertise is probably better learned through observation, not through only a sit-and-get description of the skill or strategy. The nuances are lost, during either the telling or the listening. This can cause the teacher to sound less effective than she would look if she were being observed in action. Furthermore, much of the audience typically has a foundational knowledge and understanding of the practice, skill, or strategy, so the description fails to uncover the particulars within the practice that actually make the difference.

On the other hand, observation is not only more active for the observer, but it requires more of a personal reflection than listening or observing a demonstration, which changes the learning dynamic. The observer has the ability to truly see *how* the strategy is used and can internalize the nuances. If your teachers are learning a new app for student engagement, it makes sense to introduce it in a PL session or a faculty meeting. However, if the goal is to activate peer feedback with early elementary students, it's hard to substitute actually watching a six-year-old provide constructive criticism to their writing buddy on where more detail is needed in their story, with a description of it in a meeting. The same could be said for AP literature students and every other level in between. When teachers see students being successful with a strategy, their ability to translate to their classrooms is far faster than if they merely hear about it, even from a respected peer. Hence, we find three major risks to avoid when the setting or structure of the professional learning doesn't align with its purpose.

Risk #1: Nothing Changes

If there isn't a transfer from the PL to the classroom, don't assume it's due to teachers' lack of motivation to improve. A more likely reason is that the presentation and activities within the PL weren't able to illustrate the details that make big differences. For example, having folders organized with previous work for students to use as models or the arrangement of the room that promotes student talk both have very visual applications to them. It's nearly impossible to reproduce classroom conditions like these in a PL setting without at least first observing them first. Think about other powerful moves that you want to scale among teachers, like the use of nonverbal cues to encourage students to persevere without offering help. There aren't words to describe how to do this without seeing it in action.

Risk #2: Exploiting Your Best

It might be an unnecessary uphill battle to build credibility for a teacher, who you know is the best at something, but the rest of your staff hasn't had that exposure yet. Many people in general struggle with talking about their strengths. It might be more direct to first show your staff a successful strategy in action than to invite a teacher to share it in a meeting. In some cases, when a teacher is already recognized by their peers as having a strength in a certain area, they might be able to jump right in and share an ice-breaker activity used to build classroom culture, for example. But, without already having the credibility needed to engage the whole staff, you're risking the exploitation of a teacher, which will shut everyone else down and put them in a bad position.

Be careful here. Labeling someone as an "expert" or a "master" teacher might backfire; you'll want to pause and consider your options to avoid cynicism from others. Do they need a co-presenter? Does it make sense to show a short video? Perhaps a quick read of an article on the same topic will set the stage for success. We can't say it enough – it's critical that we protect our best teachers from the risk of hurt feelings, being ridiculed, or garnering the perception that they're receiving preferential treatment. If it's a coinflip for you, and you're unsure if the staff is ready to hear from a specific teacher on a targeted topic, you don't have to make the decision alone. Your best teachers are aware of the current climate and will likely appreciate an invitation to discuss the format of PL before being added to an agenda.

Risk #3: Surface Level Learning

Finally, let's assume that this approach piques the interest of the staff. Being introduced to a new tactic or tool for teaching and learning can lead to an intrigued and curious audience. From here, some teachers might give it a try. Others might be overwhelmed with more questions than answers about how to make it work perfectly. There are some aspects of teaching that are ever-changing and refined often. A professional learning session might not offer enough depth, exploration, or experience. You probably have to revisit these topics over time, and it's helpful to consider how teachers will be supported in the interim, including how their initial learning might expand in practice.

Even though this commonly used faculty professional learning model has risks, it doesn't mean that we would never use this format or that we want our best teachers to reserve their knowledge and expertise for themselves and their students. The premise of having skilled teachers share and demonstrate their particular mastery makes sense. The challenge is providing a safe and ideal setting to create the right structure that supports adult learning.

When the best way to develop a teaching skill is to first observe an exemplary model in action, we must create conditions that allow teachers to reflect on their own teaching as they observe others so that the technique or strategy can be replicated in their classrooms. This requires a learning structure that includes observing quality lessons. To offer this cycle of learning for teachers, which includes observing actual lessons unfold, we built a model called R.O.L.E. Play that can guide your efforts for maximum effectiveness.

Investment #6: Execute R.O.L.E. Play

When we concentrate and shift our approach intentionally, considering the needs of our best instructors, we turn to alternatives to many of the traditional models of professional learning that can provide more intensive opportunities for teachers as learners. As we learned in Chapter 4, differentiated instruction should not be limited to students; our staff also needs the variety and sophistication that comes with multiple modalities of learning. To achieve this end, the acronym R.O.L.E. is intended to help you remember: Reflection, Observation, and Learning for Educators.

R.O.L.E. is a professional development structure that turns live classrooms into learning experiences for other teachers. Essentially, it creates an opportunity for teachers to witness and experience student learning by observing a particular strategy or method in practice, being performed by an outstanding teacher and/or a teacher who is doing something in an exemplary way. Quality, expert models are often demonstrated best in their natural setting – the classroom.

The purpose of R.O.L.E. is unique in that it focuses on one specific teaching strategy or learning structure. Typical classroom observation is usually broad in scope, watching a "lesson," for example. In R.O.L.E., we narrow the observational analysis and inquiry to one aspect of a lesson that the master teacher, or host, knows how to implement with precision and expertise. The essential concept is that great teaching comes from the particulars and nuances of precision in the execution of each strategy embedded within a lesson. It's not that we aren't all using effective strategies like think-pair-share. Rather, it's mindfully executing each aspect of the strategy with precision and efficacy, generating high levels of student achievement as the result.

R.O.L.E. unfolds in three phases of learning for both the host teacher and the observer. Each phase of the R.O.L.E. experience is equally important as it brings the learning full circle by providing clear *before*, *during*, and *after* learning experiences. Reflection, observation, and learning are aspects of each phase and overlap as the experience takes place. We will describe each of the sequential phases of R.O.L.E., but first, let's break down the essential features of *Reflection*, *Observation*, and *Learning for Educators*.

One quick note before we begin. We realize that this structure is quite sophisticated. We assume that this is preceded by other simple well-known practices like learning walks, pineapple charts, observe me sign-ups, teacher studies, ghost walks, classroom exchanges, and recording lessons/teacher practices to share at meetings or post to a discussion board. So many schools are engaged in this type of professional learning that we wanted to call that out. R.O.L.E. is another additional structure that supports learning for all teachers and showcases your best without putting them on stage to show-and-tell.

The Heart of R.O.L.E.
Reflection
Reflection is intentionally present in each of the phases of R.O.L.E. Play. Before the scheduled classroom visit, the host teacher prepares to share insight on the practice being observed. For example, if a classroom is selected to model the successful implementation of a jigsaw, a collaborative learning structure, the host teacher would provide some background information on the class and describe the lesson that will be observed. Through the process of articulating the details of the lesson, the host teacher becomes mindful of the intentional decisions that

led to the use of a jigsaw for this particular lesson or concept. The teacher might share the selection process of each step within the jigsaw, the structure for selecting groups, and the process for facilitating the three steps of the protocol.

What might seem obvious to the master teacher can often be the key factors that lead to success for other instructors. This is why the description of the focus strategy should happen face-to-face (rather than written communication) because it encourages inquiry on the part of the observers. That inquiry, in turn, draws the host teacher into a reflective state to deeply consider each intricate detail of the lesson. It's also of note that this isn't a mentor/mentee relationship. In fact, the observer may have far more experience than the host. The key is to focus on the execution of the strategy, not the lesson or even the teacher. This sets the stage for the heart of R.O.L.E. Play, observation.

Observation

It is the classroom visit, the observation of the strategy in action, that contributes to the unique perspective that R.O.L.E. Playing offers. During the observation, it is natural for the observing teacher(s) to make connections and comparisons between what they are noticing in the R.O.L.E. classroom, how student learning is impacted, and their own practices. Review Figure 6.2 for our Notice and Connect Observation Tool.

Recent advances in neuroscience and the understanding of our mirror neurons has demonstrated that learning by keenly observing others is a dynamic way to develop our own new specific skills (Acharya & Shukla, 2012). The normal thought pattern that leads to reflection as we observe a practice can actually lend to the development of new abilities.

It is during this in-the-moment reflection that wonderings surface, which should be intentionally brought to the debrief portion of the R.O.L.E. after the observation and posed as questions to the host teacher. However, the benefit to the observation is not limited to the observers. As the lesson plays out, the host teacher's awareness of intentional decisions is heightened. Because she took the time in the preview meeting to methodically

What did I observe the host teacher doing?	How did the host teacher's action impact student learning?	What connections am I making to my own teaching?

FIGURE 6.2 Notice and Connection Observation Tool

narrate the strategy, she can now notice the details that might have been overlooked. Both the identified observers and the host teacher are noticing with intentionality each nuance that leads to the strategy's success. Everyone is observing, everyone is reflecting. Remember, the shift here is that we're not doing this *to* our best teachers but *for* them.

Learning for Educators

The purpose of R.O.L.E. Playing, by design, is to support learning and growth for everyone who participates in the process. When candidates for a host teacher surface, the opportunity to see success in action is typically well received by fellow teachers. Since the observation is sandwiched between opportunities to discuss the strategy with open Q&A, the observers and the host teacher gain clarity on the details of the lesson. Probing questions spark wonder that leads to thorough descriptions of strategies that support student learning.

Because R.O.L.E. Playing is a professional learning structure, participants enter the experience with a perspective of growth rather than evaluation. Certainly, there are accountability factors that can come into play when a school is studying a strategy, but there is not a grade given to the teacher modeling the strategy that is being highlighted. There is always room for improvement and the R.O.L.E. Playing process provides low-stakes opportunities for growth to occur through reflection and observation. The whole point of the process is that both the host teacher and the observers, regardless of their years of experience, are moving toward more intentionality and precision with a specific practice.

Choosing a host for the observation is key to ensuring that learning will occur for everyone involved in the R.O.L.E. Play. While we are not expecting perfection, we also don't want to land on mediocrity. If teachers are going to take time to observe one another, targeting an exemplary model of a specific strategy or instructional approach is necessary. Keep in mind that just because a teacher might have mastered student collaboration using a jigsaw protocol, it does not mean she has refined the beginning and ending of daily routines to maximize instructional time within the day or class period. A teacher might surface as a viable host for one aspect of his teaching, then participate as an observer when the focus for the R.O.L.E. Play shifts. You can think of your best teachers holistically, but you can also think of which teachers are best at what.

As previously mentioned, the R.O.L.E. Play, shown in Figure 6.3, has three distinct and equally important phases to the process. In each phase, the learning is authentic and targeted, which makes the desired skills more likely to transfer than with other professional development experiences that remain at knowledge and understanding level, but don't necessarily lead to replicability. Let's unpack how the *before, during,* and *after* phases of R.O.L.E. Play work.

Phase One: Before, a Collegial Discussion About the Strategy

Collegial relationships and freedom in how to teach are hallmarks of teacher retention and satisfaction (Futernick, 2007). The first phase of R.O.L.E. Play capitalizes on both retention and satisfaction by providing teachers with an opportunity to hear a detailed description of what they will observe. An open dialogue provides observing teachers insight on the decisions that the host teacher makes and how the lesson will unfold. This conversation on the intricacies of the strategy and why the strategy was chosen also benefits the host teacher. By the end of the discussion, everyone gains greater clarity into the important subtleties

R.O.L.E.

Reflection, Observation, and Learning for Educators

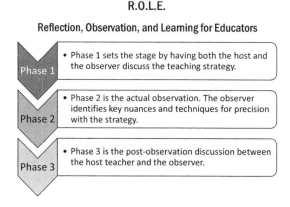

FIGURE 6.3 R.O.L.E.: Reflection, Observation, and Learning for Educators

regarding the strategy, the decision-making while lesson planning, and how the implementation should unfold. This reflective discussion is the power of R.O.L.E. and should not be skipped or cut short.

Phase Two: During, Observing the Host Teacher

This phase of R.O.L.E. Play breaks down the walls between teachers and turns the host teacher's classroom into a space where not only students learn, but fellow teachers become students of pedagogy as well. The observing teachers quietly find themselves in the classroom as keen onlookers, watching the host teacher instruct her students, using the strategies discussed in Phase One. This powerful design creates a flow of ideas, builds relationships, strengthens culture, and creates the perfect context for Phase Three.

Phase Three: After, a Debrief Between the Observer and the Host

When the lesson ends, the team reconvenes – ideally this happens immediately after the lesson, hopefully the very next period of the day. A protocol is followed to help the observer(s) discuss the strategy and what was gleaned from the observation phase. It is necessary during this time to discuss the nuances and specifics so that the observing teachers can transfer the skills into their own practice. It's likely that they already use the strategy themselves. The point is to use it with more effectiveness. This discourse provides everyone the opportunity to dissect the strategy and critically examine how it was used.

It is true that the strategy preview is set up for ample opportunity for any initial questions to get answered. However, when teachers watch the live strategy in action, they begin to notice details that they might not have thought to inquire about before they observed. Circle back to our physical therapist, Jeff. Without witnessing the series of exercises, Jeff's fellow PT might not have thought to inquire about patterns of movement, an intentional design of Jeff's workout for the patient. In the final phase of the R.O.L.E. Play, the chance for the observers to voice their curiosity is provided in this reflection meeting. A key feature is that the host teacher is present, which prevents misconceptions or assumptions from forming. Additionally, this time for debrief serves as a reflection session for the host teacher as well and includes every aspect of the P.R.A.I.S.E. Model that we will describe in Chapter 9.

Let's visit a R.O.L.E. Play led by Connie when a team of educators observed Bret Davis, a high school ELA teacher outside Detroit in Center Line, Michigan. Bret's peers were excited to visit his classroom during student-led conferences when Bret and the student mutually determined the grade for the course. Bret had been working hard to shift his class to be more standards-based and include students in the assessment process. Admittedly, he still had some hiccups to work through, but he had successfully created a system where students brought evidence of learning for the standards highlighted in each unit.

In Phase One, Mr. Davis shared with the observing teachers what he did leading up to conference day. The evidence that the students were providing in the lesson that we were observing was to support their ability to analyze how an author's choices concerning how to structure a text, order events within a text, and manipulate time to create such effects as mystery, tension, or surprise. He shared that in his experience, students struggle to stay focused on the author's choices and write about it in an analytical way versus summarizing and offering an opinion about the text.

He knew that some students will understand the standard and will be able to search their portfolios for evidence while other students will realize that they do not have evidence of their ability to master it. Fortunately, the lesson doesn't stop there for his students. They will have the opportunity to create a piece of writing that demonstrates mastery of the standard. Then, there typically is a third of that group who will struggle to wrap their heads around the overall standard and the idea of literary essays will have to be revisited as an intervention.

Students not conferencing with Mr. Davis are either conducting mock interviews with one another to prepare for their meeting with him, gathering evidence, or in some cases, they are creating evidence that will clearly demonstrate mastery. Bret wanted students to manage their time effectively, so he planned five reflective questions found below. These questions could be asked to themselves, or could be used to practice for the conference and get feedback from a peer.

1. What specific evidence do you have?
2. What does that evidence tell us?
3. Which piece of evidence best demonstrates that you mastered the standard?
4. Provide feedback to yourself or your classmate:
   a. What was the best piece of evidence they picked and why?
   b. What can be done to improve a weaker piece of evidence?
5. Offer encouragement to yourself or your partner in the form of praise for something they showcased.

When we entered the classroom, Mr. Davis had a station in the center of the room where conferences were to take place. As observers, we positioned ourselves as discreetly as possible, but still able to hear the conversation in the grading meeting. Three students brought forth their work to Mr. Davis. Each one talked in great depth about how their writing supported the components of the standard and measured up to the rubric the class developed at the beginning of the unit. Students were surprisingly honest and attuned to their weaknesses, identifying areas where they needed to grow. They used language from previous learning targets and success criteria as they talked through their pieces.

One student required Mr. Davis to ask some additional questions so she would discuss her work and evidence more. Mr. Davis kept his questions open-ended and funneled the student's attention toward what she had and had not learned yet. Mr. Davis used one of the success criteria and flipped it into a question for her. He asked, "What impact do you want the organization of your writing to have on the reader?" The young writer began giving herself feedback about how she could restructure the piece to be more suspenseful. She identified approaches such as flashbacks to accomplish the goal of backfilling information to provide a sense of surprise to the reader.

When it came time to assign a grade to her learning, the student gave herself a B. She suggested that if she were to go back and provide more complexity in the structure of the text, she would be comfortable with an A- maybe even an A. Mr. Davis asked her about recognizing this skill in other authors. She rattled off several examples of books she had read where the author successfully used parallel plots and flashbacks to create mystery and suspense. She left the meeting with a clear goal for her next steps to show she had met the standard.

After the observation, we all gathered to discuss what we saw. Mr. Davis went first to share what he expected and what surprised him. He also specifically asked for feedback about the students not interacting in the conference. He was concerned that they might not be on-task the entire time and might be spending too much time listening in on the conferences. This is Connie's favorite part of the R.O.L.E. Play, and this lesson was no exception. The debrief was casual but laser focused on gathering more information about what Bret did to generate that kind of student awareness of their own learning. Questions below started to flow from the observers who didn't think to ask them in Phase One.

1. How did students co-create the rubric?
2. Can students use evidence from other classes?
3. Why did you choose to put the conference spot in the center of the room?
4. Is it always that quiet?
5. How did you create norms?
6. What happens when you and a student disagree on the grade?
7. What if the "evidence" isn't tangible, but they can express their learning verbally?

As with most R.O.L.E. Plays, these questions prompted some responses of clarification. But other questions caused the host teacher to pause and reflect. Question four, is it always that quiet, flipped the conversation from a Q&A to brainstorming. Mr. Davis had thought the room was a bit too quiet which might make it feel that the stakes were higher than he wanted. He quickly solicited ideas from the observers on what he could do to make it more relaxed. One observer suggested quiet music, another observer circled back to the question about why the conferences took place in the center of the room. Mr. Davis then narrated his thinking aloud for us and considered the outcome of moving the conferences away from the rest of the class so students didn't feel like their peer conferences would be disruptive to the teacher–student meetings taking place. They all agreed that the quietness as a norm supported student concentration and was central to the scenario, something that Mr. Davis hadn't thought about too deeply and something that the observers would implement in their classrooms.

As a result of this R.O.L.E. Play, the observers were able to debunk some of their beliefs that students are not able to fairly and honestly assess their own learning and Mr. Davis was able to use the questions of his peers to gain his own awareness about a detail that likely had a greater impact on the climate of the class than he previously considered. The final outcome of the R.O.L.E. Play was learning and clarity for both the observers and the host, something that our best teachers deserve and a far better result than what we get when we put them in front of the faculty to describe their new grading and conferencing structures.

Maximizing Your Investment: Conduct Action Research

An additional role that educators should embrace and that administrators should support, especially within our best teachers' classrooms, is that of researcher. This positions the school to maximize the knowledge and expertise of the staff by using action research in the school setting. We need to know and understand more about what works and what doesn't – who better to answer those questions than those on the front lines through action research?

Too often, we look to the outside for answers that we can find right within our own school walls, among our own staff. We need to identify the qualities and skills of our best teachers, learn as much as we can from them, and then transfer that to their peers. Our best teachers ignite powerfully positive *feelings* in their students, we know what the kids *say* about them, and how our parents *react* to the success of their children. The challenge is in translating those feelings, words, and reactions into concrete teacher growth and student learning outcomes in every classroom.

That said, something that can maximize your investment in R.O.L.E. Play is to turn your best classrooms into laboratories to test your theories, pedagogical approaches, and curriculum materials. Your action research can be as complex or simple as you want it to be. Consider our desire to transform classrooms into spaces where teachers are directing and guiding learning and students are learning from one another through collaboration.

Start by picking something to study. Let's use jigsaw as an example. Hattie's (2012) meta-analysis points to an effect size of 1.20 for jigsaw. Elliot Aronson, the inventor of the popular student collaboration strategy, developed a three-step process (Aronson et al., 1978). Step one is the expert group, where students gain an understanding of only one aspect of a multi-faceted concept of the learning. Step two brings students from each expert group together to share their learning piece with the intent of creating the full picture through dialogue. Step three, an often forgotten step, returns students to their expert groups to process together what they gleaned from the second phase. It is during this third and final phase that students gain clarity on how their piece fits in with the other pieces to develop the complete context and solidify the concepts.

Education is rich with strategies, and the key is to implement the strategies with expertise and fidelity. Using a teaching technique like jigsaw requires thorough planning and preparation and highly structured learning time. By opening up master classrooms to other staff, we can begin to study and learn how the strategy is chosen, organized, and executed. Understanding the different variations and methods of use to determine which tactics and nuances have the best outcomes is critical. We couple this with R.O.L.E. Play because the way in which we use a strategy when we know it's effective is exactly what we want everyone to observe as it unfolds in real time.

If we want our teachers to leverage the full potential of jigsaw, or another strategy, we have to be certain that our implementation is of the highest quality. Otherwise, we run the risk of another "been there, done that" mentality of poor implementation of highly effective strategies that get thrown in the "that doesn't work" pile.

We liken this to the relationship that Pooja Agarwal (researcher) had with Patrice Bain (classroom teacher) when they studied retrieval practices and their outcome on student learning. They describe their work in *Powerful Teaching* (2019) whereby the actual student results improved through the use of certain strategies over others. We believe that this is the "proof" that some educators need to reinforce the fact that all students need access to "what works."

How R.O.L.E. Play Profits the Whole System

The benefits of R.O.L.E. extend beyond your superstars. It's likely they will be candidates to host some of these experiences, modeling quality instruction in a structure that provides reflection for them. However, they can also benefit from observing other teachers showcasing the practices mastered by their colleagues. There are four steps to follow to get R.O.L.E. Play started in your school.

Step #1: Identify Your Potential R.O.L.E. Play Teachers

You can get started with R.O.L.E. Play in your school with ease. The first thing to do is to reflect on and identify the key areas where teachers are having success. Remember, you're looking for pockets of excellence in a classroom that you would like replicated elsewhere. R.O.L.E. Playing focuses on a very specific aspect of a teacher's craft. Here is a list of popular R.O.L.E. Playing focus areas:

- ◆ Routines/Structures
- ◆ Classroom management
- ◆ Ice breakers, warm-ups, or launch activities
- ◆ Blended learning
- ◆ Systems of community building
    - ◆ Restorative practices
    - ◆ Morning meetings
- ◆ Formative assessments

- ◆ Cooperative learning structures
- ◆ Instructional strategies
  - ◆ Programs and projects (Student Podcasts, Readers' Workshop, etc.)
  - ◆ Student-centered learning (Socratic Seminar, PBL, etc.)
  - ◆ Questioning techniques
  - ◆ Feedback scenarios

Use Figure 6.4b to brainstorm a list of your best teachers and the area of focus that each of them might R.O.L.E. Play, for visitors in an effort to replicate their greatness more widely.

Step #2: Build Excitement

Any new initiative must be supported, well communicated, and viewed as valuable among the staff. R.O.L.E. Play, by design, empowers teachers and if communicated well, can garner excitement and interest. An initial step is to gauge your faculty's willingness to visit peers as a way to reflect, observe, and learn as educators.

Your R.O.L.E. Playing will be most successful when you have teachers who voice an interest in learning more about a specific component of teaching and commit to implementing it in their classroom. Mandating that teachers participate in a R.O.L.E. Play exercise can diminish the positive impact that the process has for both the visiting and host teachers. In order to provide alignment between staff interest and the host teachers' areas of strength, it will be helpful to determine if interest already exists and what you will need to do to create it. A simple interest survey, like the one in Figure 6.5, gives teachers a voice and gauges buy-in at the outset of your initial plans to put it into place.

Possible R.O.L.E. Host Teachers	
Teacher Name	**R.O.L.E. Focus**
Mr. Finch	Kagan Structures
Mrs. Kelley	Blended Learning: Station Rotation

FIGURE 6.4a Example of Brainstorming Chart for R.O.L.E. Play Teachers

Possible R.O.L.E. Host Teachers	
Teacher Name	**R.O.L.E. Focus**

FIGURE 6.4b Brainstorming Chart for R.O.L.E. Play Teachers

R.O.L.E. Play Interest Survey

Name: _____

If we were to offer a R.O.L.E. Play in our school, how interested would you be in being an observer? Check all boxes that apply.

☐ Yes! I'm definitely interested! Sign me up today!

☐ Yes, I'm interested now if the focus is relevant to me.

☐ Yes, I'm interested to learn now from/with specific individuals.

☐ Yes, I'm interested, if I can have some input on when it will be scheduled.

☐ In the future, I'm definitely interested.

☐ I would like more information about R.O.L.E. Plays before I commit.

☐ I have enough information about R.O.L.E. and it does not interest me, regardless of the topic, team, or time.

Are you willing to be a host for a R.O.L.E. Play? (Select one.)

☐ Definitely! I already have an idea of what I could share.

☐ I would be willing to be a host if there was interest in observing my classroom.

☐ If I were asked to be a host, I would probably be willing.

☐ I would like more information about being a host before I commit.

☐ I would be willing to be a R.O.L.E. Play host, but I have some conditions that would need to be met.

☐ I have enough information about R.O.L.E. Play and I would prefer not to be a host.

☐ Other: _____

Some of the topics considered for a R.O.L.E. Play have been brainstormed in our school. How interested would you be in participating with a R.O.L.E. in the following areas?

	Definitely interested	Might be interested	Definitely NOT interested
Peer Conferencing	☐	☐	☐
Co-Constructing Success Criteria with Students	☐	☐	☐
Restorative Circles	☐	☐	☐
Student Managed Classroom Routines	☐	☐	☐

FIGURE 6.5 R.O.L.E. Play Interest Survey

What R.O.L.E. Play focus would you like to see in our school, and who would you like to observe implementing it?

_____

_____

Comments/Questions about R.O.L.E. Play:

_____

_____

FIGURE 6.5 (Cont.)

Step #3: Maximize Opportunities

Time is one of the most valuable resources within a school system. The implementation of R.O.L.E. Playing will require us to rethink how teachers spend their day. Because teachers will need time before the observation to discuss the lesson, time to observe a portion of the lesson, and then time for reflection afterwards, schools will need to create space throughout the day and possibly before and after school for this effort to be successful.

Creatively finding ways for teachers to have rich discussions on the lesson is critical. Introducing R.O.L.E. into the culture of the school forces administrators to rethink how professional learning communities are structured, whether or not teachers will have non-instructional duties, how substitutes or interns can be used to "free up" a teacher, and how the master schedule can be designed to support peer visits. Every school is different so brainstorming new structures to embed R.O.L.E. Play in the culture is essential.

Step #4: Practice R.O.L.E. Play Protocols

The best R.O.L.E. Play experiences begin with the host teacher's ability to draw attention to certain aspects of the strategy. But, many of our best teachers do not realize that their instincts, which have been refined and mastered over time, are often what set them apart from other educators. The ability to narrate their thoughts improves the quality of the R.O.L.E. Play and increases the opportunity for replication in other classrooms. This is why reflection protocols and sentence stems can help. Setting up systems for things like who goes first, what types of questions to ask, and the look-fors during the observation make the process smooth, efficient, and more effective.

The Bottom Line

Harnessing the skills of your best teachers, and replicating them within other classrooms so great teaching permeates your school, is central to improving student performance. The catch is for the expertise to be learned in a productive and active manner so that it is diffused throughout. This requires a very particular method of professional learning that benefits both the expert teachers and those teachers poised to learn.

A passive approach, the sit-and-get model to skill development, with teachers idle and disengaged, is simply ineffective. R.O.L.E. Playing creates a system designed to support everyone's growth by opening authentic and engaging spaces for teachers to collaborate and share best practices that have been discussed and actually observed.

This growth won't occur overnight, but the nuanced teacher development we are describing is directly aligned with the flywheel effect. Through continual effort and persistence, over time, the massive heavy flywheel begins to move and eventually momentum begins to take hold (Collins, 2001). Excellence in teaching is developed through collaboration and collegiality. An analysis of expertise execution through real-time observation and pre- and post-reflection conversations raises everyone's performance through a thorough understanding of what techniques are most effective and why. This takes us back to Dr. Jeff. He becomes more mindful of his own practice as he prepares to share details of his evaluation. His trainee simply can't learn to conduct the physical tests in an effective way unless Jeff describes the intricacies of the work, demonstrates how to do it on real patients, and answers questions about the *how* and *why*, not just the *what*.

HOW TO MAKE YOUR INITIAL DEPOSIT

Implementing the R.O.L.E. Play will take a bit of planning. You'll need to secure subs for teachers to observe the teachers identified as model classrooms. But you can get started inviting teachers to observe one another. One popular way to welcome teachers into one another's classrooms is by using a Pineapple Chart described by Barnes and Gonzalez (2015). It is a calendar where teachers can invite each other to visit their classrooms to observe. The chart is posted in a central location so teachers can indicate when their lessons will include instructional methods that other teachers may be interested in seeing. It can be as simple as an interactive online tool, introducing a new learning center, or as complex as a Socratic seminar. When another teacher sees something on the pineapple chart they are interested in observing, they visit the classroom. They can stay for five minutes or the full hour. There are no scheduling conflicts if teachers can observe during their planning time. But reassigning subs to cover classrooms during their planning time is another way to free up a teacher or two to pop into a classroom they are interested in observing.

7

Applying Data Informed Feedback

The Difference for Kendra

Over the summer, Kendra attended a school-based workshop about how to engage students in quality conversations to establish a more student-centered classroom. When fall arrived, she was fired up and prepared to facilitate learning protocols so students could engage in productive struggle. She wanted to make this the year that her students would be doing more work than she was – as the saying goes – never work harder than your students.

The students in Kendra's class had been introduced to *accountable talk stems*. Things like, "I agree/disagree because…" There was an anchor chart dedicated to several examples/suggestions of how students might respond to one another during class discussions and they were encouraged to reference it, even use the stems verbatim. Kendra knew that developing a culture where conversation flows freely starts with listening and contributing to others' comments. Many second-grade teachers might be satisfied with students talking to students and completing group tasks together. But Kendra, as a superstar, knew her students were capable of more and was determined to find a way for their conversations to be more natural.

Connie had led observation teams in many schools before, but this was her time working with the cohort in the Michigan

DOI: 10.4324/9781003321316-7

school. Kendra was the first teacher to host a lesson. Prior to visiting Kendra's classroom, Connie inquired about the lesson and asked Kendra if there was anything specific the cohort members could notice or observe for her. Kendra was pleasantly surprised. As a veteran teacher who had been rated as "highly effective" for several consecutive years, she'd never been asked this before. Typically, the observation process was not much more than an affirmation that she was doing okay or she should simply keep doing what she's doing. Connie's inquiry caused Kendra to think about the data that she wished she could collect when she was busy teaching.

To achieve her goal to engage students in rich conversations where they interact more with one another than with her, Kendra reflected on the past couple of days recalling what was working and what wasn't. She recognized that in the class discussions students were using the talk stems, but it felt forced. When she approached collaborative groups, it seemed like her presence prompted students to use the talking strategies. She wondered how they interacted when she was not listening to them. A more natural dialogue was what Kendra was striving to activate in her classroom. She shared this goal with her colleagues and Connie.

Connie inquired with some reflective and clarifying questions to understand Kendra's goal. She asked the following questions:

- ◆ What speaking and listening skills do your students already have?
- ◆ What is a reasonable amount of conversational exchanges you'd like to see currently?
- ◆ What would an ideal small group discussion look like?
- ◆ How are students successful in their conversations?
- ◆ Why might their interactions be limited?
- ◆ What type of data would be helpful for you to use for next steps?

This exchange between Connie and Kendra took place as the other cohort members listened and offered their own wonderings and suggestions for data collection. Connie and the team suggested that they gather the following data and share it with Kendra after the lesson:

◆ How many ideas are started during the group discussions?
◆ How many comments or questions follow the initial idea or topic?
◆ What type and how many ABC (Agree, Build, Challenge) comments are used?
◆ What type and how many questions are posed by students to other students?
◆ What causes an idea to fizzle and move on to another idea?

Kendra was a bit nervous but more excited to finally have a perspective she wasn't able to gather on her own. She could never hear how students interacted when she wasn't around. She had given them exit tickets to reflect on how effective their conversations were, but after today's lesson, she would get hard evidence.

When the team arrived for the lesson, they positioned themselves so she could hear multiple groups working. They scripted what she heard from each group and created charts to easily capture data. When Kendra approached a group, the observer made a note that the teacher was near. Then they paid extra attention to note how the conversations went after Kendra walked away. Most of their notes were dictation of what the students said and some tally marks to count the comments and topics.

After the lesson, everyone paused and took time to reflect on the data they collected and prepare for dialogue. They compiled and summarized it so it would be easy for everyone to review together. Some of the key noticings that the team shared are shown in Figure 7.1.

The debrief of the lesson was a conversation. Each observer shared the data she gathered and encouraged Kendra to share what she noticed and her reflections about it. The ABC comments were surprising to Kendra. She knew that students were using the talk stems but hadn't thought to pay attention to which ones they used more freely. Clearly, each group struggled to build on one another's thinking and ideas. Kendra knew she needed to

	Group 1	Group 2	Group 3
Ideas shared	3 ideas in 10 minutes	7 ideas in 10 minutes	15 ideas in 10 minutes
Number of Add-Ons per Idea	Range: 3–10	Range: 0–4	Range: 0–2
Type of ABC Comments	Agree: 60% Build: 5% Challenge: 35%	Agree: 80% Build: 2% Challenge: 18%	Agree: 90% Build: 0% Challenge: 10%
Types of Questions	Clarifying Justification Perspective	Clarifying	Procedural
Fizzlers	Transitioned to new topics naturally.	Transitioned to new topics naturally. Conversation stalled and quieted.	Students shared one at a time, almost a round robin format.

FIGURE 7.1

encourage them to build on thoughts and grow ideas collaboratively. She was going to emphasize this in future lessons, but wasn't convinced that would be enough. Connie shared that students didn't seem to have quality listening skills. Another teacher offered to send a link to a fantastic blog that talked about how to develop active listening strategies to help Kendra build those skills for her students.

After the debrief, Kendra felt empowered, informed, and supported. She was more motivated than ever and recognized that without the team's data-based feedback she might not have ever noticed that the poor listening skills were the root cause for mundane student-to-student talk. Because Connie established the purpose of the visit by asking Kendra about a goal, Kendra's interest and motivation to receive the data from the team was high. It also meant that she came away with something to do and the support of the blog for how to make it happen in a subsequent lesson.

 ## The Costs Associated With Over Flattering Feedback

Across the United States, over 90% of teachers are rated as effective or highly effective (Wiggins, 2015). In some states, the number

118 ◆ Applying Data Informed Feedback

is near 100% (Educator Effectiveness, n.d.; Dynarski, 2016). Is it true that every teacher in a given state is a rockstar or even that 90% are at the top of their game? We don't mean to be skeptical, but our time collaborating with schools, leaders, and teachers suggests the number is less than what teacher evaluations report. In order to be rated this high, the feedback teachers are getting would have to be powerful, based on evidence, and highly practical for making improvements. And, the evidence of learning and student outcome data that came with it would match or rival these percentages. That's not the case.

To leverage the potential of evaluation tools, many of them were overhauled, while others continue to be modified. The aim is that they are professional growth tools that move away from a "gotcha" or one-and-done event, but rather an ongoing, sophisticated measure of a teacher's skills, knowledge, and abilities. No easy feat. The evaluation instrument itself must be able to effectively capture these areas.

One of the most widely used is the Charlotte Danielson Framework for Teaching. As of 2013, the "FFT Evaluation...was adopted, approved, or adapted by 31 states and over half of the country's 20 largest school districts." The framework organizes teaching into four primary domains: 1. Planning and Preparation, 2. Learning Environments, 3. Learning Experiences, and 4. Principled Teaching (Danielson Group, 2022a, 2022b). Other tools used in schools, such as Marzano Teacher Evaluation Model and 5 Dimensions of Teaching and Learning, have similar categories for reviewing how teaching aligns with research-based best practices.

The domains are comprehensive and capture critical aspects of effective teaching. Despite the contention around evaluation tools, we want to acknowledge that they hold incredible insight into the professional learning needs of teachers at all skill levels. We acknowledge that it is hard to use the same tool for evaluation and coaching, but that is precisely how they should be used. Each observation holds the key to an incredible amount of qualitative data that can be used to influence professional learning for individuals and groups of teachers. The data transforms the tool into a skills inventory. Yet, we rarely view teachers' abilities through stages of skill acquisition as described in Chapter 3. Even when we think a teacher is good, we must ask, "good at what?" Teacher evaluation data can provide rich insight on the skills and abilities of individuals and the collective whole.

The issue isn't with the evaluation tools themselves. As a matter of fact, 93% of teachers agree that the teacher evaluation system is intended to promote teacher growth and development (Prado Tuma, Hamilton, & Berglund, 2018). So why do so few teachers attribute professional learning to the feedback they receive from school leaders (Hunter & Springer, 2022)?

Here's the real problem: regardless of whether the teacher is considered a superstar, a backbone, or a mediocre, they say that the feedback received from their supervisors is most often unhelpful. The teacher evaluation process guarantees that teachers will receive feedback, but it doesn't speak to the quality, value, or usefulness of that feedback. If observing and evaluating teachers is a once-a-year obligation for school leaders, and it's crammed between every other responsibility, it's easy to see why many teachers find little value in the process.

In our work with teachers, we hear comments about feedback that are concerning. The superstars share that feedback about their instruction is generic, and they typically leave with the idea that what they're doing doesn't need to be changed. An example might be, "You have great student engagement." The mediocres agree that the feedback is generic, and they often add that it's unactionable. It might sound like, "You need to increase your student engagement."

These two examples of feedback could be classified as affirming or critical, perhaps you prefer the terms encouraging or constructive. Whatever you call them, they don't offer much in terms of how to improve or what to do to continuously grow. Plus, the language is subjective. How do you define "engagement"? What does it mean to be "great"? To what level are we making an "increase"? These undefined buzzwords do little to give our superstars the support for growth and do nothing to tell our mediocres how to improve. Too much of the feedback that our teachers receive is basically useless.

"Keep up the good work." This is the message that many of our superstar teachers get when it comes to reflecting on the quality of their instructional practices. The fact that administrators are voicing this type of "praise" tells us that some teachers in their schools are absolutely rocking it. Students are learning. Parents are pleased. Achievement is through the roof. Leaders wish that every classroom were staffed with teachers like these. However, the lack of quality feedback leaves these teachers on their own, potentially sending a message that status quo is good enough. And, we put "praise" in quotations because "keep up the good work" barely constitutes anything that we would support as feedback or praise (more on this in Chapter 9).

We don't believe that this is the message school leaders intend to send. Yet, it's exactly how it is received. Why do so many superstars get overlooked when it comes to getting the coaching or consulting they need? It's usually one of the following three reasons:

1. Focus is placed on teachers whose instruction is ineffective, instead of the best teachers.
2. There is a perception that constructive feedback is negative and our best teachers are doing just fine.
3. How a teacher with great instruction could improve is not obvious to the person tasked with providing the feedback.

For these three reasons and others that we're sure come to mind for you, we developed our P.E.A.C^2.H. Model so that school leaders can begin to invest in their best teachers the way that they deserve. You'll see how the model works and why it matters for the whole school.

Investment #7: Share Feedback Using P.E.A.C^2.H.

Generally, we find that our best teachers soak up, reflect upon, and respond to effective feedback more than any other group. Backbones are content with what they're doing, and mediocres are often oblivious. The best teachers, on the other hand, are constantly thinking about their pedagogy, reflecting on how it impacts student learning, and seeking new ways to continuously grow. How we communicate with teachers about their instruction varies. There is an abundance of evidence on the impact that feedback can have when done well (Marzano, Pickering, & Pollock, 2001; Hattie, 2008; Wiggins, 2012). Various researchers list characteristics of effective feedback. See if you can identify some commonalities by looking at Figure 7.2.

Given the importance of improving teaching and learning, we think it's fitting to begin by looking at ways that leaders can use a model for feedback that will provide data and partner with teachers in a way that the best teachers crave, which will encourage them to continuously improve. Feedback works, but only if you use a model for delivering that makes your feedback effective. George du Maurier, Franco-British cartoonist and author said, "An apple is an excellent thing – until you have tried a peach" (Du Maurier, 1894 p. 157). We would like to introduce you to the P.E.A.C².H. sequence for feedback. Its sequential six-step process provides transparency, encourages a collaborative partnership between teachers and the people providing feedback to them, and can be used in both formal and informal settings.

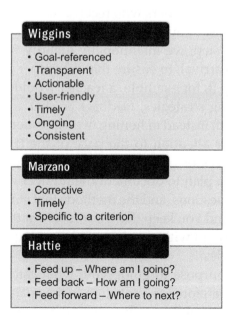

FIGURE 7.2 Characteristics of Feedback

Step 1 – Establish the PURPOSE: *Set Clear Intentions of Focus Before the Classroom Visit*

Prior to visiting a classroom, whether it is a formal evaluative observation, a walkthrough, or a structured process like instructional rounds, it is important to define the focus for some of the instructional or curricular elements that you will consciously notice during visits. The guidance for where to target your attention can come from school or district initiatives, professional learning, the teacher's professional goals, or even a particular curiosity that you have about the teaching in your classrooms (like the amount of time students are given to discuss material in their own words).

Instructional leaders who partner with teachers to identify and/or communicate specific look-fors in classroom observations are exhibiting transparency. When we stay true to focusing on the predetermined agreed upon areas, a level of trust is earned. Going into a classroom without communicating or asking the teacher about an area of focus, equates to classroom teachers failing to share a learning target or lesson purpose with the students. As Chappuis and Stiggins (2017) say, "students can hit any target that they know about and that stands still for them." It's no different for teachers who receive feedback on their pedagogy. The purpose should not be a mystery.

In this first step, we intentionally identify what we plan to notice, prior to arrival, to ensure that we gather the specific data we are seeking. If, for example, a teacher would like to improve their questioning strategies, feedback in that area becomes the primary focus. If, instead of honing in on questioning techniques, you divert your attention to the pace of the lesson, important details and pieces of questioning evidence will go unnoticed. However, if you plan to document the number of questions, the quality of the questions, and the methods that students engage in the questions, and you keep that your focus for the visit, you will leave the classroom with concrete evidence of questioning from a variety of angles.

Without a purpose to guide you, what catches your eye is arbitrary and therefore may not align to the goals your system or your teacher has established. Even with the purpose, we still have to discipline ourselves to stick with it. Because of the extremes of a lesson, everything from classroom management to the use of a video can draw our attention away from our focus. We can't let that happen if we truly want to gather that data necessary to provide feedback on something that matters for our teachers.

Step 2 – Gather Usable EVIDENCE: *Collect Qualitative and Quantitative Data Without Judgment*

When the purpose of a classroom visit is to follow up with useful feedback, the more evidence collected, the better. Consider how you might collect both qualitative and quantitative data. Quantitative data is evidence with numeric value – events and moments that can be quantified and measured. Qualitative data is non-numerical data that is descriptive. Figure 7.3 provides examples of quantitative and qualitative notes from a lesson in the areas of engagement and questioning.

Area of Focus	Quantitative Evidence	Qualitative Evidence
Engagement	When the teacher was reading to the class, ten students were tracking the text, eight students were looking at the teacher, two students were looking around the room, one student was sharpening a pencil, and one student left to go to the bathroom.	While the teacher was reading to the class, the teacher paused and engaged the students in a think-pair-share. Students verbally made predictions about what would happen next in the story.
	During the 50-minute reading lesson, 33 minutes were spent engaged in the text; students listened to the teacher read for 22 minutes, read with a partner for 4 minutes, and independently read for 7 minutes.	While the teacher read to the whole class, students were reminded to follow along in their texts. When reading with their partners, the listening partner followed along.
Questioning	During the mini lesson, the teacher asked 42 content questions and 12 student management questions.	During the mini lesson, the teacher used questions to direct student behavior like "What should you be doing right now?"
	The teacher asked 11 original questions and when students didn't respond to a question, the teacher posed a follow-up question within less than 2 seconds.	The teacher asked follow-up questions to offer a hint or cue to students when the right answer wasn't given quickly.

FIGURE 7.3

During the gathering phase, both types of evidence should be factually based on what the person observed and not their interpretation. The raw data is analyzed in the next step. Observation notes that are objective are most helpful for both you and the teacher. Rather than describing the level of engagement as "high," use quantitative data. For example, you might record that 22 out of 25 students were looking at the teacher, two students were trying to find their Chromebook chargers, and one student had their head down. These types of notes open the door for dialogue. The student with their head down might have an understanding with the teacher about coping methods. It's also possible that the teacher is having a hard time reaching that learner. Those two scenarios call for completely different teacher and observer responses.

Gathering evidence and data will require keen observation skills and sharp attention.

This means that observer behaviors such as roaming the room and interacting with students should be closely monitored since they will prohibit you from gathering whole class data. Limited data makes crafting quality and useful feedback challenging. There are times when your primary purpose for being in a classroom is to be visible or make student connections. When preparing to provide feedback, these connections and visibility become secondary for the duration of your observation. This allows you to give your full attention to the lesson and notice even the smallest efforts a teacher makes.

Circling back to the example of the teacher focused on questioning, if you spend the majority of your time consumed on the one student with their head down, or the students looking for chargers, your evidence of questioning patterns will be limited. It's important to honor the agreement made with the teacher and gather observations in the area of focus. Additional data can be collected, but not at the expense of the focus.

Step 3 – ANALYZE Your Data: *Review Evidence After an Observation or Walkthrough*

Analyze the evidence from the lesson by reviewing and reflecting on the data you collected. Align it to the goals you and the teacher agreed would be the focus. Exceptional or concerning areas outside the area of focus should also be shared, but never instead of or to overshadow the feedback identified in Step 1.

Step 3 is your opportunity to look for patterns and areas of strength aligned to the focus. Very often there are outliers in your data, but the primary focus is on the preponderance of evidence. This identifies what is likely to happen most of the time. Both teachers and observers tend to notice the outliers but for your teachers to grow, especially your best teachers, it is vital to identify the critical nuances observed related to the area of focus. Keep isolated incidents in perspective, while the majority of the evidence focuses on the effective strategies and techniques the teacher utilized to maximize student learning. Nuances matter in the classroom, but we're only addressing the nuances associated with the focus area. Our goal is to drill down in one area deeply versus addressing the vastness of the overall lesson. Once the data are analyzed, you're ready to either coach or consult or a little of both depending on the conversation.

You can also analyze the data for areas that a teacher might not notice themselves, sticking with the focus of course. For example, maybe a teacher's focus is on student-centered learning and during the observation you found that students asked the teacher twelve questions during a small group task. You notice that eight of the twelve questions were answered by the teacher when they could have posed additional questions in response to the students' questions to help build and develop learner autonomy.

In the case when your purpose is to focus on maximizing instructional time, as an additional example, there may be pieces of data you notice and simply want to call to the teacher's attention so they can reflect on it for themselves before you offer your thoughts. Please note that you should avoid asking questions where you expect the person to read your mind. Ask genuine, thought provoking questions or simply share the data collected. For example, if the transition time to the carpet took twelve seconds and the transition back to their work spaces took sixty-four seconds, just share those numbers with the teacher. If the teacher is able to analyze their data with you and come up with their own ideas, you're using their thoughtfulness to help them process the lesson themselves. The awareness alone will trigger coaching, if the teacher has some solutions of their own or consulting if some suggestions are needed.

When analyzing the data collected in Step 2 and directly connected to the area identified in Step 1, be careful not to assume that your best teachers have all the answers. They get stumped sometimes too. This is the power of open dialogue and communication with a predetermined area of focus. You will work together through the process to find possible solutions or in some cases, you simply offer tools, resources, or suggestions to help the teacher grow.

Steps 4 and 5 – Provide COACHING and CONSULTING: *Provide Both Reflective Questions and Quality Suggestions*

Notice we have combined two steps here. Coaching and consulting are not separated because the one that comes first will vary. However, it's not combined into a single step because both are necessary for quality feedback. Let's get a clear understanding of the difference between the role of a coach versus the role of a consultant when it comes to providing feedback, especially with your superstars.

Coaching With Superstars

When you're in a coaching mode, you'll likely be asking more questions than not. The coaching approach is explorative. You will commonly engage in this role with your best teachers because a coach holds the belief that the teacher has the expertise and knowledge to solve their own problems. Do not make this same assumption with mediocre teachers or even your backbones. But, your superstars' needs are different. With just a little guidance to uncover a problem, your coaching will help them to also discover solutions.

In their cognitive coaching model, Costa and Garmston (2016) suggest five steps: 1. posing invitational questions, 2. paraphrasing, 3. posing clarification questions, 4. pausing, and

5. presenting data. We want to point out that using questions to help your teachers reflect is only one aspect of the equation. In fact, using questions alone is not effective. It's important to note two things.

First, we're using questions *after* analyzing data, not as a blanket approach, as in "how do you think the lesson went?" or "what might you improve next time." Even your best teachers will struggle with totally open-ended questions like these and they don't specifically funnel reflection on the area of focus and main purpose for the feedback as identified in Step 1.

Second, quality reflection requires more than just thinking about what you did or how you did it. Cognitive scientists are now clear that people don't reflect well on something while they're doing it. They are more successful with support from a coach or consultant to process the meaning of evidence from an observer, data collection, video, partner, etc. (Willingham, 2009).

Let's take a closer look at how this method unfolds when you're acting as the coach.

Posing Invitational Questions

Using invitational questions is a strategy to begin a two-way conversation that results in the teacher identifying what stands out to them, what they perceive as problems, and what they are trying to achieve with the lesson. Critical to the success of the conversation is that it begins with a reflection on something other than memory. Using the teacher's memory alone can lead to misinformed impressions of how the lesson went or, worse yet, disagreements and defensiveness. That's why we collected the data. Take a look at the prompts below.

◆ As we look at the questions I scripted during the observation, what level would you say most of these are based on the model we use? (Be sure to have a DOK chart or Bloom's Taxonomy for reference.)

◆ What have you gleaned from the evidence you collected in the exit ticket about how well they understood the content?

- ◆ As you reflect on the tally chart that you created for student participation and discourse, what do you see regarding your students and their opportunities to engage? (Note here that the teacher knows far more about the students and their willingness to participate than an observer ever will.)
- ◆ When you look at the amount of time you spent on each of the chunks in the sequencing of the lesson, does it reflect the amount of time you planned?

Remember, we're only picking one area of focus so you wouldn't ask all of the four questions above. These are meant to be samples of how you would use data to start the conversation. After the teacher reflects objectively on the evidence, you can move into more open-ended questions like, "what could be done to increase the rigor and cognitive level of your questions now that you see that they're mostly recall?" Your best teachers are able to solve problems on their own, but it's better that you show them the problem rather than tell them about it, which should be inverted for your backbones and mediocres who don't typically benefit from this type of coaching model.

Paraphrasing

The back-and-forth of your professional dialogue, when done well, also lets the teacher feel valued and heard. Active listening will demonstrate that you understand what they said by sharing a summary of what you heard. This is an important step because it is easy to misinterpret what is being said. This happens because they're either not explaining their ideas well or you're not gathering an accurate account. Do not skip this step; it is vital that you use the paraphrasing technique to be on the same page. Here are some examples of how it might sound:

- ◆ After listening to the teacher reflect on the data…"What you're saying is…"
- ◆ After listening to the teacher pose a question…"What you're wondering is…"
- ◆ After listening to the teacher make a suggestion for the future…"It sounds like you would…"

♦ After listening to the teacher set a goal…"The biggest priority for you is…"

Posing Clarification Questions

Clarifying questions help get specific with goals or challenges that the teacher is facing. They are not leading. Their purpose is to probe more deeply to get to the heart of an issue and reveal the focus.

♦ What else can you say about that?
♦ How did you come to that idea?
♦ How did you arrive at that conclusion?
♦ What might be some other options or alternatives?
♦ Who might you go to for support with that?
♦ Did I paraphrase what you said correctly?

Pausing

Processing time offers the teacher space to think and reflect before responding. When exploring ideas, options, and alternatives in a coaching role, the teacher will need some time within the meeting to think aloud or silently. Be comfortable with letting them think quietly so they can fully reflect on the lesson. It's important to realize that they have not processed the lesson based on your observational feedback yet. We can't assume that their reflection is on the same information, which is why reflection with support bolsters teacher growth. That's why this model is so important for your best teachers because it is the mutual connection over sophisticated nuances within the classroom that they may otherwise not reflect on.

Presenting Data

As we described previously, having physical evidence allows for you and your teacher to review it together. Instead of your thoughts being compared to their thoughts, together you develop an understanding of what the data shows. Pay attention to the teachers' responses when you present data. You will vary the number of reflective questions and suggestions as you toggle between coaching and consulting. Start with some open-ended questions to get the conversation started, then determine when it's time to shift to consulting.

- ◆ What stands out to you?
- ◆ Where does this data fall compared to your goal?
- ◆ How does this evidence align with what you were noticing as the lesson unfolded?
- ◆ What other evidence might we need to draw real conclusions?

Consulting With Superstars

Your role as a consultant is to help them solve a problem using your understanding, knowledge, experience, or resources you have access to that they don't yet. Your mindset when you are in a consulting mode is to be focused on how to improve the teacher's practice in a specific area. You're thinking more about the problem or goal than you are about the individual. When you're coaching, you're exploring the teacher's thoughts and expertise; when you're consulting you're partnering with the teacher to add your thoughts and expertise to the conversation.

Consulting doesn't mean you have all the answers or you have a sure-fire solution to the teacher's biggest classroom problems. It does mean that you're recognizing that some outside resources might be necessary in order for the teacher to move on to the next level. In the next chapter, we will outline new ways that a consulting conversation can continue outside of the two of you. Stay tuned for that, especially when you're not fully equipped to make substantive suggestions. But, let's not diminish the power of being an observer. If you zoom out in your focus on the prearranged area to the one big thing that the teacher can do differently that they're not seeing as the person who's trying to manage a planned lesson, then you should just reveal what that is and discuss it.

It might seem like your best teachers don't need consulting, after all, they're the best, right? Still, even your superstars value feedback in the form of consulting. It could be an article that offers suggestions, an example of another classroom where you saw someone else tackle a similar scenario with success, or a strategy that you know will work better. Wiggins says that feedback must be *actionable*. Marzano uses the term *corrective*, and Hattie suggests it provides clarity on *where to next*. In every case, the giants in education identify some sort of consulting that is needed in order for feedback to be most effective. Yes, it's okay for you to tell your teachers, even your best teachers, what they could do differently. Candor is kind.

In some cases your consulting will be delivered more as an expectation, as in the case of a teacher who allows students to line up by the door four minutes before the end of class. In other cases, it will be shared as an option. You will invite them to try something to see if it works or helps. If it doesn't work the first time, that's where Step 6 – our next and final step – of the P.E.A.C².H. Model comes into play.

Step 6 – Establish New HABITS: *Offer Continuous Support and Encouragement to Build and Maintain Effective Habits*

A single annual observation with a feedback session is hardly enough to make an impact for teacher growth. However, it also doesn't mean that every time you visit a classroom, you're setting a new purpose.

Once your teachers have identified an area of focus or two, accompanied with action steps to continuously grow, your role continues in the form of supporting them to implement and reflect on their action steps. Building an environment keen on reflecting on the success of the strategies they will try and when necessary, establishing a new default in how they approach instruction is the pursuit. When a better way to support student learning is discovered, the goal is to establish that as an instructional habit.

The idea is that new best practices are established as a norm for planning lessons and the inferior method is abandoned. For example, instead of class discussion following a standard process of the teacher posing a question, students raising their hands, one student responding, and so on (Hamilton, 2019), we might switch to a new standard where everyone responds to the teacher's question using whiteboards. Is hand raising never going to be used again? Of course not, we just don't want that ping-pong approach to class discussion to be the only method.

Here are a few ideas about supporting teachers with new habits:

- Providing additional information like articles, blogs, or websites.
- Connecting the teacher with other professional educators.
- Outlining next action steps to fortify the new habit.
- Checking in to be sure the plan is followed.
- Inquiring about how implementation is impacting teaching and learning.

The important thing to remember is that your support and interest goes beyond the debrief of the observation in helping to bring the ideas to life. And, along the way, you may realize the need for a Yoda (we'll clarify what we mean by this in the next chapter).

Maximizing Your Investment in P.E.A.C².H.: Build and Sustain New Habits

In order for a strategy or solution to be shifted to a habit, barriers to success must be removed or reduced. James Clear, author of *Atomic Habits* (2018), suggests five strategies for building new habits.

1. Start with an incredibly small habit.
2. Increase your habit in very small ways.
3. As you build up, break habits into chunks.
4. When you slip, get back on track quickly.
5. Be patient. Stick to a pace you can sustain.

For teachers who are trying to build better instructional habits, the following five adaptations of Clear's (2018) habit-building strategies are helpful to keep in mind as you support a superstar teacher to make a shift. Let's say that a teacher is trying to improve student discourse in the classroom.

1. Start with an incredibly small habit.

   There is a touch of biology involved in why a habit should start small. When animals achieve success, dopamine is released in their brains. Dopamine is what causes you to feel good after accomplishing something. It controls pleasure (Juárez Olguín et al., 2015). When the goal is small and it's achieved, the teacher's brain helps by giving a jolt of "heck yeah," which encourages the behavior to be repeated.

   In order to increase the amount and quality of student talk, there has to be an awareness of when these opportunities exist. The teacher might start out with teaching students how to comment on one another's thoughts using an ABC tool. After a student speaks, a peer can A – add on to what was said, B – build on a peer's idea, or C – challenge someone else's thinking. A small habit is doable, and very small. Examples include:

   ◆ Prompt students to use ABC before a class discussion.
   ◆ Hold or post an ABC poster during a class discussion.
   ◆ Label A, B, or C talk to call attention to when it happens organically.

2. Increase the habit in small ways.

   Now that the exposure to ABC is in place, the teacher can increase the habit. James Clear (2018) suggests a 1% gain. Instead of calling attention to ABC once per lesson or about six to ten times per day, they might set a goal to increase that number by one. The added prompts for ABC talk could be before a class discussion as a goal, within a class discussion as a reminder, or at the end as a reflection. It could be as simple as inviting students to use the strategy by asking, "Who would like to ABC on Nolan's comment?"

The longer-term goal is to build the habit in both the teacher to allow for ABC talk, but also for the students to engage in this type of conversation with automaticity. Making it *the* way class discussions work.

3. As you build up, break the habit into chunks.

Once the teacher is consistently implementing the strategy and forming it as the new habit for how they teach and students learn, you can look for ways to leverage this as an asset or strength. Perhaps the ABC strategy is applied in an ELA lesson, but not as frequently in a math lesson. Or, at the secondary level, it's possible that ABC is solidly initiated at the beginning of class but not as much during or after the discussion. Here are some chunks to consider when helping a teacher build their habit.

   ◆ Before, during, or after the lesson.
   ◆ During whole group, small group, or individualized instruction.
   ◆ With specific groups of students (high/low, introvert/extrovert, front/back seating, active/passive, etc.).
   ◆ During specific times of the day or week.
   ◆ Within types of lessons (review, foundational, extension, etc.).
   ◆ During different teaching times (launch of the lesson, deliberate instruction, scaffolding, partner time, actively learning tasks, independent application, lesson closure).
   ◆ Within stations as students rotate.

With the application of a new, more effective habit, success will surface in chunks. It typically starts in a single area like a subject area of elementary teachers or as part of the lesson for secondary teachers.

4. When you slip, get back on track quickly.

Embracing a growth mindset should not be something we just instill in our students. As educators, we need to employ the strategies and thought process just as much. Educators take teaching and learning very seriously. For most, being an educator is part of our identity since many feel like it is a calling. That means that when something doesn't go perfectly, we tend to get down on ourselves and can even get defensive.

Acknowledging that a strategy or an effort to shift to a more effective strategy and make it a habit fell short with limited success, can be perceived as a failure. When Kelly Clarkson sings "What doesn't kill you makes you stronger," the words may seem accurate but science has a different spin. Negative events actually increase the likelihood of failing again at the same task, and sometimes we fail even harder in subsequent attempts (Shpancer, 2010).

If this sounds discouraging, then you'll agree that it takes deliberate practice for teachers to avoid slipping back into safe and familiar methods. For any teacher, even your best, to abandon their effort to establish new instructional habits, takes time and support.

5. Be patient and stick to a pace you can sustain.

The gradual release of responsibility framework builds in an assumption that as learning occurs, learners (in this case teachers implementing an instructional change) assume the responsibility over time. As your teachers apply new methods and develop better instructional habits, they are likely to need support. We have included ways to offer that support in this book that doesn't depend on you to be the sole source.

Personalized professional learning – Chapter 4

Participating in external programs – Chapter 5

Peer observations and feedback – Chapter 6

Outside experts – Chapter 8

Your role as an instructional leader is to follow through as your teachers establish new habits with on-going interest and support when needed. Your teachers are bound to experience fluctuations depending on their needs. Use Figure 7.4 as a guide for how you can support teachers to build and sustain new habits.

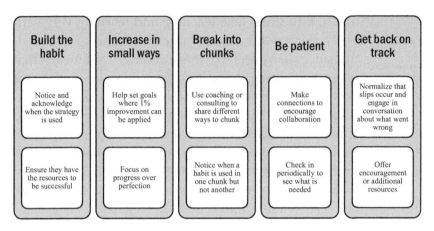

Build the habit	Increase in small ways	Break into chunks	Be patient	Get back on track
Notice and acknowledge when the strategy is used	Help set goals where 1% improvement can be applied	Use coaching or consulting to share different ways to chunk	Make connections to encourage collaboration	Normalize that slips occur and engage in conversation about what went wrong
Ensure they have the resources to be successful	Focus on progress over perfection	Notice when a habit is used in one chunk but not another	Check in periodically to see what is needed	Offer encouragement or additional resources

FIGURE 7.4

👥 How P.E.A.C².H. Profits the Whole System

To apply a growth mindset, there must be a challenge faced. Without a worthy goal, targets are easy to achieve and the thrill of accomplishment is diminished. Since your teachers hold different strengths and needs, their goals will be unique to each of them.

Schoolwide and district goals are not to be ignored, but how they are achieved will differ from class-to-class. This is where individuality comes into play. When everyone is challenged and working to grow, a culture of improvement breathes within your school setting. Conversely, if your best teachers are left to do their own thing all the time, the message that learning and growth matters becomes inconsistent.

In his book *Make it Stick: The Science of Successful Learning*, Peter Brown (2014) shares that for information to be stored in our brain and retrieved for use in future scenarios, we need to apply effort by applying the new information. In other words, in order to successfully establish new learning and new routines, there must be some struggle.

Don't misunderstand this. We aren't promoting that you make teaching difficult for your staff by throwing roadblocks in their way. Establishing struggle isn't just about making something hard. It's about setting goals that are worthy and require effort to accomplish. When you apply the P.E.A.C^2.H. Model, you are able to identify what every teacher needs, including your superstars, so you and your staff model the same lifelong learning we strive to instill in our students. Let's review the benefits shared in Figure 7.5 that apply to everyone in your school.

Whether you're working to elevate your best teachers or those who need more support, this six-step model provides a consistent process for you to apply. You'll establish a shared purpose for an area in which your superstar teacher is going to grow. It could be classroom management basics or, for your best teachers, it might be strengthening peer feedback using success criteria – whatever the agreed upon goal is when you visit that classroom. You will know exactly what to notice as it relates to the teacher's goal, which sets you up for the subsequent conversation and the impact that you'll have on your best teachers' work. Then your observations can expand to other areas for feedback.

The data you collect will connect you with the teacher as you analyze together. Key points of data are used to eliminate an us/them perspective. Instead, together, you work to address the teacher's pain points and tweak teaching to enhance student learning.

Your ability to adjust the balance of coaching and consulting provides differentiated feedback for all of your teachers. Some educators will position you as the consultant and as you'll discover in the next chapter, your superstars might exceed your expertise and require their consulting to be provided by someone other than you. Either way, every teacher in your school will engage in a valuable feedback session that causes them to know exactly how they can improve their instruction to increase student learning.

With the identified action steps for how to make a positive impact on the learning in a classroom, the P.E.A.C^2.H. process shifts to continuous support in the form of developing habits. Since your focus is on growing pedagogy with small habits, every teacher in your system has an individualized action plan that describes exactly what is needed for growth. The message this sends is that everyone can improve and that improvements are incremental. The students are not the only learners in the

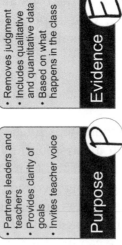

Purpose P
- Partners leaders and teachers
- Provides clarity of goals
- Invites teacher voice

Evidence E
- Removes judgment
- Includes qualitative and quantitative data
- Based on what happens in the class

Analyze A
- Aligns data with goals
- Fosters reflection
- Limits subjectivity
- Sytematically processes evidence

Coach/Consult C
- Sparks reflection for the teacher
- Positions the leader as a problem-solving partner

Habits H
- Creates action
- Offers consistent support
- Makes room for change that sticks

FIGURE 7.5

building; we are all constantly and forever learning. Professional learning requires sustained learning and practice over time (Wei et al., 2009). Therefore, the time and permission to build new habits that lead to more effective teaching and learning is needed for every teacher. And, when backbone and mediocre teachers get the message that the best teachers are also focused on improvement, it levels everyone up a notch or two.

Feedback should not be perceived by teachers as a single session or meeting. Reflecting on instructional practices and developing or sharpening methods is part of a bigger process. The P.E.A.C^2.H. Model uses data, collaboration, and a growth perspective so that ideas and strategies will be embraced by the teachers. When they see that the process will have a positive impact on the way that they teach and how students learn, everybody wins.

The Bottom Line

Observing teachers and providing feedback is one of the essential jobs we have as school leaders. Just going through the motions to comply with a teacher evaluation tool is a waste of time and energy for everyone involved. Our six-step model for effective feedback using P.E.A.C^2.H. provides a process that fosters transparency, acute observation information, intentional reflection on what was noticed in a lesson, roles for initiated teacher reflection and contributing to their growth, and follow-up to ensure the teacher is properly supported.

Our best teachers deserve a robust process that pushes them to look for ways they can continuously grow. Inviting them to join you in each step along the way communicates that you care and you're interested in their success and ultimately the success of the students. It's this type of challenge that leads to a feeling of achievement.

The best teachers often get tasked with projects or responsibilities that their leaders believe they are capable of taking on. Perhaps this is why offering a goal to improve the instruction of teachers who are already successful can be passed up.

Given the number of educators who are leaving the profession and the amount of criticism they face day-after-day, including what they bestow upon themselves, it seems unkind to deny them the joy of growing and enhancing their passion for teaching. The P.E.A.C².H. Model makes it possible to use feedback in a way that celebrates growth and makes working in your district valuable for your best teachers.

HOW TO MAKE YOUR INITIAL DEPOSIT

There's no need to wait to begin to include data informed feedback. Begin to collect qualitative or quantitative data then share that with teachers. To get your feet wet and transition teachers into discussing lessons based on evidence, start looking for and sharing what's working. If the teacher has tight transitions, time the number of seconds it takes for students to gather at the carpet; or in classrooms with older students, a teacher might consistently visit each student during independent work time, so you can count the number of students who receive one-on-one attention and maybe even the number of times. Starting with glowing data will be a smooth way to practice gathering this type of evidence, will give teachers more experience reflecting on objective details from the lesson, and will hopefully spark their interest in having more data-based dialogue about their instruction.

8

Searching for Yoda

You'll Never Look Your Best Without Dayal

Dayal Baxani is the Yoda of the clothing industry. He's a haber-dasher by trade. And, unfortunately, not too many people know what that is anymore. Before department stores, and even cloth-ing stores in general, someone had to measure and make your clothes for you. That person was a craftsman – a haberdasher. The profession of haberdasher or the person who operates a haberdashery is almost nonexistent today, and most people don't need someone to make their clothes anymore unless it's a for-mal ceremony or another rare occasion. Instead, most people buy garments off the rack and have them altered if necessary. But, Dayal's clients aren't *most people*.

In an age when you can get your clothes delivered to you in a subscription box and can send back what you don't like, Dayal's services go in the other direction. While a haberdasher can design clothing for any gender, Dayal specializes in men's attire. His team measures every aspect of a man's build and marks all of his personal preferences and then creates a wardrobe from scratch. His suits are completely customized, including the lining, which could be anything from a pattern of skulls to vintage guitars to a company logo. He can even embroider special stitching of his client's choice inside of the fly front zipper fabric.

DOI: 10.4324/9781003321316-8

Dayal comes from a long line of people who have done this work. His father is a haberdasher. His mother's father designed, cut, and sewed suits from scratch, no machine, all by hand. His eye for fashion is impeccable, and his ability to put colors and patterns together is genius.

Of course, most people will never use a haberdasher. You don't have to call a haberdasher if you're content buying your clothing already made. But, Dayal's clients are looking for something special that requires the Yoda of men's fashion. They've been to the department store. They know how to pick out a nice belt. But, they're looking to take their personal look to a new level. When we interviewed Dayal about his work, he said, "I want the outfit that I design to be part of your motivation in the morning. It's your personal uniform that you should get excited to wear when you get dressed."

He went on to talk about how clothing is as much psychological as it is physical. Everything from the button design to the thread color matters. He focuses on the finer details so that the men who experience his efforts receive nothing but the best, and they come back because they feel like champions when they wear the clothes he designs for them. Men don't go to Dayal as a mediocre dresser or someone who couldn't care less about how their jeans are tapered. They find Dayal when they're already at the top of their game, but they know that they could present themselves even better. They search for the Yoda of men's clothing when the quality and refinement that they seek simply cannot be found in a regular department store, no matter how nice it is. The precision and craftsmanship comes at a price – time and money – but it's what the best-dressed men do when they want to dress even better.

 ## The Costs Associated With the Leader As the Sole Expert

Most of the principals or assistant principals we work with support and evaluate more than 20 people, sometimes doubling or tripling that number. This responsibility is often spread over multiple disciplines, spanning various content areas, and grade levels, including highly specialized teaching staff. One might think that this could be a recipe for disaster, given that these supervisors are unlikely to have expertise in all of the areas that their teachers cover, but that's not the case. By honing and combining the right skills and abilities, leaders can overcome any lack of expertise that they might have in the areas that they oversee. But, there's often an elephant in the room about this very topic. Too many teachers and school leaders still believe that their evaluation skills worsen the further they get from the subject or grade level that they taught. It's simply not true, in *most* cases.

We will attempt to debunk the myth and empower our leaders: you don't need to be a subject matter/grade level expert to lead people to do their best work. There are numerous other professions where it isn't even feasible for the boss to be an expert in all the areas that they oversee. Great leadership is not about what the leader knows and can do anyway; it's about empowering people to reach their full potential (Frei & Morriss, 2020). That said, there are important skills that school leaders need, especially when they supervise teachers who teach a subject or grade that's foreign to them. Let's enumerate these skills based on evidence and research in the field of supervision.

First, as a supervising observer, as long as you *understand the context* in which the work is done and are *willing to listen* to what the people find to be effective, you can both learn more about their roles and empower people to get better in them (Mathur, 2019). As such, the first leadership skill of a non-expert supervisor is *listening* and then acting upon what you hear. The bad news is that "less than 2% of all professionals have had formal education or learning to understand and improve listening skills and techniques" (Llopis, 2013). The good news is that listening is a skill, which means that we can all advance in our ability with training and practice. Fortunately, we can all improve our listening skills with explicit instruction and intentional practice. That said, leaders who are adept listeners can effectively oversee people with a particular expertise that the leader doesn't have. The skill to hone is not what you're supervising but rather your ability to listen to better understand the context of what you're about to observe or just observed in a classroom.

Second, letting all employees, especially your best, set their own goals and targets is paramount to effectively managing people when you don't have their specific knowledge or background. The critical factors, says Gallo (2011), author of the *HBR Guide to Dealing with Conflict at Work*, are to make sure that the goals are connected to the organization's broader objectives, to take ownership in ensuring that employees can achieve the goals they set, and to incorporate any personal interests that the employee might have that are linked to their professional goals. But Gallo also warns that employees shouldn't set goals alone, that high performers, especially, need feedback to meet their goals, and that you can't ignore failures as part of this model. This is precisely why the P in our P.E.A.C². H. Model focuses on identifying purpose for observations and feedback.

In education, a great deal of our supervisory models actually call for a collaborative goal-setting process between the supervisor and the staff member. What this means for school leaders as supervisors of content areas or grade levels that they never taught is that collaborative goal-setting with feedback toward the goal can make for an effective supervision structure. Getting better at this process is more important in most cases than learning more about the science or art lesson that the teacher teaches.

This is where the third strategy for supervision comes into play, and it's the one that we like the most because it's the easiest to learn about and implement. It's a focus on instructional best practices. It's true that there are general strategies that work across all genres of pretty much any organization, especially in schools where effective strategies for teaching, leading, and intervening have been studied through research and evidence in practice. Take, for example, a high school math teacher who becomes an assistant principal and now oversees the social studies department. Teaching math is different from teaching social studies, particularly when we consider the content knowledge one needs to teach either subject. But, there are highly effective teaching strategies that work across both disciplines that the supervisor can use to strengthen classroom instruction through observation and feedback.

Let's just say that the social studies teacher needs to increase the amount of student talk time in his classroom. As a teaching and learning strategy, it has to be baked into a lesson plan for it to work. Many studies, including Hattie's Visible Learning MetaX online reports, have found that class discussions demonstrate a greater effect for learning than many other strategies. The former math teacher (now supervisor) may use discussion strategies and formats as the basis for observation and feedback to improve the experience for students in the social studies teacher's classroom. This same concept applies at the elementary level. If a former fifth-grade teacher becomes a principal, they can still support primary teachers as well as art, music, physical education, and special education.

There are any number of instructional strategies that our mediocre, backbone, and even best teachers can get better at executing with precision. Using *the strategy*, which is connected to instruction, not *the content area*, provides a platform for any supervisors who haven't taught the subject matter that they now oversee.

Myth debunked. School leaders need to listen to the context of what they're observing, set collaborative goals with feedback toward their attainment, and study instructional strategies that work the best across all disciplines. If you're reading this book, it's because you want to support your *best* teachers, but you just learned about the three primary ingredients in support-ing *any* teacher, especially the ones who teach something that you never taught. Simply put, the notion that teachers can't be effectively supervised by someone who doesn't know their content area is a myth – one that we should all quit accepting because it may be used as an excuse by teachers who are reluc-tant to accept the feedback that they are receiving. If content is actually in question, supervisors have people to look to for support.

But, let's be clear, there are cases where elements of the myth hold weight. The problem isn't whether or not a non-subject matter expert can supervise *the average* employee. The problem is whether or not the supervisor can effectively improve the skills of *the best* employees. The best employees don't just need a good listener, a collaborative goal conference with feedback, and a supervisor who knows what great teaching and learning looks like.

When it comes to Steps 4 and 5 in the Coach and Consult aspects of the P.E.A.C^2.H. Model from the previous chapter, our superstars need more. These special people may need a subject matter/grade level expert in a particular area that they want to improve. The best teachers won't get better at the rate you want them to just because you listen, set goals with them, and suggest strategies. They need more. They need a Dayal – a Yoda – the master craftsman that can elevate a person's game.

It's hard to believe that someone wouldn't know the story of Yoda, but just in case you don't, he's about 2 feet tall, green, and the most skilled Jedi Master in the movie *Star Wars*. When Luke Skywalker needs to learn the ways of the Force, he learns what he can from Obi-Wan Kenobi, but there's a turning point in his training, and he needs more. The average Jedi, and Jedis are already considered above average in the world of galactic battling, can learn from their master, but Luke was unique. His training required a master of all masters. He needed Yoda, and so the story goes that he went in search of him, which made the difference in his Jedi skills.

This is true for teachers too. The best way to train a master is to employ the skills of an even more powerful master. Even though skilled leaders can supervise people outside of their expertise, the only way to actually observe and effectively improve the practice of a champion, the best teachers in your school, is to find someone who matches or rivals their specific expertise. One of Yoda's most notable qualities wasn't just his incredible power within the Force himself, it was his role in the recognition and growth of other Jedi Masters. Although disappointing, whether or not you're a Star Wars fan doesn't matter, the metaphor underscores the need for next level training and coaching. Your best teachers are Jedi Masters, and the only way to improve the skills of a Jedi, the strongest Jedi, is to find Yoda.

Let's use an example. Suppose one of your best teachers is your Band Director. She's an expert in music development, and her command of the classroom is outstanding, despite the more than 50 students on the risers. In most other classrooms, you have something in your mind that can improve the teaching or the environment or some other factor. For this teacher, your mind is blank. There's no doubt that this teacher can improve – everyone can – and these individuals often crave feedback. You just don't have any to give. Time for a Yoda. A more powerful master could also be one that has more knowledge in a focused area such as questioning skills rather than content or grade level – but the same concepts apply.

The troubling shame of it is that developing our expert teachers is a long-overlooked problem. Not only is it typical to ignore our best teachers as not needing our help, we tend to only observe them due to the compulsory nature of the supervision system, often with an already understood notion that we won't improve their efficacy in any substantial way. This line of thinking skips over the critical aspect of the P.E.A.C^2.H. Model where teachers are engaged in quality conversations, including deep reflection and concrete suggestions for continuous improvement.

The irony is that these are the teachers with the greatest potential to improve and the greatest influence over the improvements that their peers can make. The supervisors of these shining stars are typically cast under a spell, believing that their best teachers can't reach any higher than they already have or accepting the false premise that there's nothing that can be done to help them grow. It's not a productive state of mind. We must accept that it is our role to support the growth of *all* teachers, even and especially our best teachers. This puts us on our journey toward finding Yoda – an obligation that we have when we seek to invest in our best.

You might be asking yourself this important question: but how am I, a non-subject matter expert, supposed to identify a Yoda and bring them to my school to train the Jedi Masters? The first answer is that you just might not find one. That doesn't mean that you quit looking, and sometimes the way to find Yoda is to ask your Jedi Masters who they consider to be the Yoda (in your district or in the edu-world in general). You might not get the incredible mathematics professor and reformer, Jo Boaler, to observe and provide feedback to your superstar math teachers, but you can certainly try. And, there might be a mathematics expert in teaching at your local college or university who may be just waiting to hear from a school for support with something like this. The point is that there are a number of strategies for finding Yodas so that your Jedi Masters learn and grow in ways that they wouldn't without the expert help.

Investment #8: Find Y.O.D.A.S.

We are using the acronym Y.O.D.A.S. (shown in Figure 8.1) to describe the process for identifying the value you bring to your teachers, even the best ones and where their needs exceed the expertise you currently have. If you and your best teachers target a specific area for focus, your next steps include finding resources to encourage continuous professional learning and that might lead you to look beyond the typical tools that are used to support your best teachers.

Your Strengths

Any leader who hasn't already conducted a strengths assessment should do so. Just Google a leadership strengths assessment or leadership inventory, and you'll find a number of them. A leadership strengths assessment can provide you information to use for reflection or something you can use with a coach

FIGURE 8.1

(if you have one). We like iMap Strategic Solutions because of the team features, and the Natural Leadership Profile (NLP) from Higher Performance Group, just to name two that are available. The iMap tool comes with a cost; NLP is free online. Every leader should have an inventory of their strengths as a leader. But, what we're aiming at here is not just about leadership; it's about *instructional leadership*.

You should know your strengths and weaknesses as an instructional leader so that you can continue to grow in the areas of instruction that will help you to support your teachers. There are four categories, shown in Figure 8.2, that we would like to call out as having significant importance for anyone who supervises

Instructional Strategies
- Am I familiar with the research about pedagogy and instructional strategies?
- Do I know which authors and studies to reference when it comes to pedagogy in the classrrom?
- What am I reading to improve my knowledge of instructional decision-making for teachers?

Content Knowledge
- Am I familiar with the standards that need to be addressed in this grade level and content area?
- Do I know the curriculum materials and resources well enough to comment on their usage?
- What am I referencing to improve my knowlege and understanding of the standards and curriculum?

Grading and Assessment
- Am I familiar with the research and academic literature on grading and assessment practices?
- Do I know which authors and studies to reference when it comes to grading and assessment practices?
- What am I reading to increase my knowledge and understanding of how teachers' grading and assessment practices can support students' academic achievement and well-being?

Teacher and Student Dispositions
- Am I familiar with the research on restorative practices, responsive classrooms, and other methods of creating human-centered classroom environments?
- Do I know which authors and research to review when it comes to teacher and student dispositions?
- What am I reading to expand my knowledge of these topics?

FIGURE 8.2

or observes teachers. Teachers should be working on these four areas, and they'll do that best with a coach who is working to improve in them as well.

Instructional Strategies

Every leader who supervises teachers must know the instructional strategies that work the best to support student learning. We need leaders to know how to collect evidence of student learning *and* teacher quality. As an aside, we believe that the pendulum has swung too far towards what students are doing. It's true that the old models of observation were too heavy on the teacher's action, but a balance is critical. Planning and preparation are still the hallmarks of an effective lesson, and teachers make decisions about the strategies that they plan to use to engage students as the lesson unfolds. We want those decisions to be backed by sound reasoning and clear research. And, looking for evidence of student performance and learning is imperative too. Effective instructional leaders strike the balance.

Take, for example, the fact that Hattie's MetaX demonstrates that the jigsaw method has an effect size of 1.20. This is an important finding for instructional leaders to know and understand. You actually don't need to know much about effect sizes and meta-analyses. Effect size is just a nice way to say, the-bigger-the-better, and meta-analyses are simply the compilation of a number of research studies, which is better than one-off findings. Over three hundred influences have been studied. The result is that nearly all of them work. The trouble lies in not knowing which influences are more effective than others. The average effect size of all influences is 0.40. This is what Hattie calls the "hinge point." Anything above 0.40 is better than average. Anything positive that is below the hinge point is still effective, just less impactful than many other influences on student learning (Hattie, 2021).

That means that our jobs as instructional leaders are to know and understand the strategies, like jigsaw, that are above the hinge point and can accelerate learning because of their effects. Here are a few questions to ask to evaluate your level of skill with instructional strategies:

1. Am I familiar with the research about pedagogy and instructional strategies?
2. Do I know which authors and studies to reference when it comes to pedagogy in the classroom?
3. What am I reading to improve my knowledge of instructional decision-making for teachers?

Content Knowledge

Having content/grade level knowledge in all areas of teaching and learning is practically impossible. School leaders who were former teachers have an advantage in that they at least have content knowledge in the subject matter that they taught, but even that can be tricky. For example, years of teaching algebra doesn't necessarily equate to a deep understanding of calculus. This is true of grade bands as well. Tons of experiences with fourth-graders doesn't provide much perspective on teaching kindergarten, even though the two grades may be housed in the same school. Nonetheless, not having a deep knowledge of a specific content area or grade level, as we've discussed before, is not a deal breaker for quality supervision. Especially if your knowledge and understanding of instructional practices are strong, you can get away without a deep knowledge of the content you supervise.

That said, consider the difference between being fluent in another language versus being conversant. People who are fluent in Spanish can read, write, and speak it with ease. Those who are conversant in Spanish can get along by ordering from a menu, holding a basic conversation, and getting to the bus station without help. There's a pretty big difference. Leaders who supervise a content outside of their expertise should work to become at least conversant in that content. Here are a few questions you can ask to assess your comfort and skill in a particular content area:

1. Am I familiar with the standards that need to be addressed in this grade level or content area?
2. Do I know the curriculum materials and resources well enough to comment on their usage?
3. What am I referencing to improve my knowledge and understanding of the standards and curriculum?

Grading and Assessment

Grading and assessment practices are a hot topic, and we're confident that they'll continue to be contested, reformed, and reimagined at every level for as long as this book is in print. We're also confused as to why more progress isn't occurring within the realm of grading and assessment strategies as an aspect of school and district equity plans – a concept for a different book. Grading and assessment practices are important for school leaders to review and study so that we can help to support how teachers are grading students and the types of assessments they use to inform instruction.

It's important for you to understand your strengths as it pertains to grading and assessment. You're somewhere on the continuum between expert and novice. The following questions are designed to help you self-assess your ability to challenge teachers' grading and assessment structures to make changes that will ultimately lead to better student outcomes. Making improvements to grading and assessment practices has the ability to improve equitable outcomes (Feldman, 2018), students' sense of belonging (Sackstein, 2021), actual achievement (Guskey, 2019), and more.

1. Am I familiar with the research and academic literature on grading and assessment practices?
2. Do I know which authors and studies to reference when it comes to grading and assessment practices?
3. What am I reading to increase my knowledge and understanding of how teachers' grading and assessment practices can support students' academic achievement and well-being?

Teacher and Student Dispositions

Teacher and student dispositions don't get the attention that they should. As for our definition of teacher and student dispositions, we're referring to any and all behaviors that both teachers and students display within the classroom setting. This includes classroom management strategies, restorative practices, voice-and-choice, responsive classroom, and other aspects of learning that occur in the classroom from day-to-day and minute-to-minute. We contend that educators ought to pay more attention to our working knowledge of how students and teachers interact to support learning and well-being. Sure, most preservice teachers take a course in classroom management, but there's far more nuance to behaviors (both student and teacher behaviors) in the classroom that support the learning process.

Some school leaders are adept at taking notice of these types of interactions in the classroom; others are not as practiced in this area. Teacher and student dispositions can include the way that a teacher uses proximity to squelch a misbehavior or even how the teacher calls on students when a question is posed. These actions are often windows into a teacher's philosophy toward management and student behavior. We're not proponents for the clip-up and clip-down system in elementary schools, but we have seen teachers use it effectively to support a positive learning environment. We're also not advocates of the long lecture in secondary schools, but we've witnessed students who are captivated as learning who benefit from this approach. It's all about *how* the teachers and students interact and our level of skill at noticing it. You can ask these questions to help assess your ability to see, hear, and experience teacher and student dispositions:

1. Am I familiar with the research on restorative practices, responsive classrooms, and other methods of creating human-centered classroom environments?
2. Do I know which authors and research to review when it comes to teacher and student dispositions?
3. What am I reading to expand my knowledge of these topics?

Obvious Gaps

We're not looking for obvious gaps in what our best teachers need. For the Y.O.D.A.S. Model, we're looking for obvious gaps *that we can't fill* as instructional leaders. That's why the Your Strengths assessment questions should lead you down the path to understanding more about where you have gaps to fill in your own supervisory leadership skills. We already know who the best teachers are, but we're not always certain about what they need. That's why we're looking for obvious gaps, which are far more easily recognized in ourselves than what we can uncover by observing our best teachers. Remember, we've already determined that we're unsure if we can help them grow in the first place or else we wouldn't be searching for Yoda.

Your gap will become obvious when you know very little about the research, you're unsure of which authors to consult, or you're not really, or haven't ever studied, one of the four areas in Your Strengths assessment. It should be obvious, too, that if you're finding true weakness in more than one area, you need to support yourself to grow as well. The habit development process described in Chapter 7 also applies to school leaders. The point here is not that you're going to select all four areas to target for your best teacher, but that you identify the one or two areas that you're not able to do on your own. That's the reason why we need to find Yoda. Now that you have one of the gaps in your sights, we need to determine the target.

Determine the Target

Determining the target is done collaboratively with your best teachers. Remember, collaborative goal-setting is one of the three important practices to support the people you supervise. We're going to target an area of your weakness as we look for our Yoda, but these areas are broad enough that you'll want to narrow it down with the help and insight from your best teachers' advice.

First, set up a meeting to discuss Your Strengths assessment with your selected superstar. Review your strengths and weaknesses that you've self-identified. Be sure to provide clarity at this meeting (or before) that your intention is to help the teacher grow but that you want to find a "more expert" person to help. Next, discuss which aspects of your weakest points could be places where the teacher can grow if someone with more expertise would intervene. It's inevitable that the teacher, who is likely very reflective, will have input into the target area of focus. Last, decide on as specific of an area to target as possible.

Consider one aspect of the curriculum or one instructional strategy to improve. No one can improve in all areas of instruction at once, not even your best teacher. An example would be one of your best teachers who desires to improve in their use of student discourse as a learning strategy when you're not the best person to help with pedagogy of that kind. The resources needed to begin the improvement process come next.

Access to Resources

Before you even search for Yoda, let's talk about building a bank of available resources for teachers, especially your best teachers. Teachers love great resources, but we find that they're always looking for them on their own and even purchasing them with their own money – don't get us started about educators using their personal money to pay for what they need to do their jobs effectively (more on this later). In this section, we're going to provide you with two tips that all of your teachers will appreciate and that will help with the specialty areas that we've uncovered in your assessment, which are the targeted areas from above.

First, if you don't have one already, create a library for teachers. You can repurpose some of the shelves in the student library, use a faculty room, or reimagine an already useful resource closet. Lots of schools have resource rooms for teachers so this isn't a novel concept. The difference in how we want to spin it – our first tip – is that you should categorize and label the various sections within the room. For example, one of the categories can be "grading and assessment" whereby teachers can find all kinds of current resources for learning about and doing grading differently.

We want to think about the supplies in our resource room with two lenses: teacher learning and student learning. Some of the resource categories are there to support teacher learning and other resources are there for teachers to use with students. If you want to be a pro, and you have the space, turn this room into a lounge and make it a fun space to hang out. One last thing before we tell you about our second tip, make sure that one of the categories is teacher leadership and their role as teacher leaders. We'll say more about this in our Maximizing Your Investment section later in this chapter.

There are plenty of quality resources available online as well. Articles, websites, and other helpful tools can be collected in a Google Drive, saved on a Padlet, or linked from a professional learning homepage your teachers can access. What we love about this option is that it's free, it can be accessed from anywhere, and your teachers can contribute to the collection when they find valuable resources as well.

Second, make a commitment to listen to teachers about the types of resources that they think they need. This isn't just so that you can add new resources to your resource room; it's so that you can prevent teachers from using their own money for supplies whenever possible. We find it shameful that an already under-resourced and under-funded profession allows its under-paid employees to buy materials so that they can do their jobs well. That said, you can't solve this problem on your own, but most school budgets have some money allocated for supplies in a way that can mitigate the amount of out-of-pocket expenses that teachers end up accruing during the school year. When your top teachers have engaged in professional development, have access to resources, and make every attempt to get better, it could be time to search for Yoda.

Search for a Yoda

Now it's actually time to search for your Yoda. Note that there was a lot of preparation done prior to conducting the search. Not all Yodas are the same. You need to know and value the skills that you require in a Yoda, and your best teachers don't need Yodas in areas where you can help them. They need Yodas in the areas that fill the gaps between your knowledge and skills and the ones that can support their growth. Let's look back to the D in Determining the Target from our Y.O.D.A.S. Model. We'll expand upon the improvements to student discourse as an instructional strategy whereby you're not the most capable person to help. By the way, that's okay. You can't be an instructional leader to the highest degree in every area. Be reminded that your vulnerability in admitting this, especially to your best teachers, goes a long way with trust, which has leadership benefits beyond your relationship with this teacher.

We're going to search for a student discourse Yoda. Where should we look? Let's take a look at the 4Ps of a Yoda Search.

People: We always look for people first. An internal search is best. Are there people in the district (teachers at other schools) or central office (specialists, coordinators, and supervisors) who are considered experts in the area that you're looking to support? Maybe you have a social studies specialist who is gung ho about student discourse, has a reputation of doing it well in the classroom, and makes it a focus of their department. Even if they're not "the guru" on the subject, bringing in a district leader, like a central office support person, has its advantages. If their knowledge, skill, and background match your needs, move forward with a meeting that will allow your best teacher and their new support person to set some goals and schedule observations.

Programs: We believe in people over programs any day of the week. But, some specialty programs are very supportive for specific changes. You'll have to do a search, but, as an example, Kagan Cooperative Learning Structures are specific strategies to support student discourse in the classroom. Its program offers all kinds of ways to engage, and the result is models for setting up structures to get students talking. Quality and research-based programs, like Kagan, are great when you need help supporting your best teachers in an area where you aren't an expert and they need expert help.

Products: Sometimes there are products associated with the area that we're targeting for improvement. A product might be a toolkit, a resource, a technology, etc. Specific to student discourse, we would point to TeachFX as our example. It has tons of features, but to simplify an explanation of what it does, it's an artificial intelligence tool that records lessons as they unfold to produce a report about talk-time in the classroom – who's doing the talking and how much of it, including silence? Products like this one support the area that you're targeting and do so without support from you. The Yoda doesn't have to be a person; as long as your resource has expert knowledge and advice for your best teacher to use for reflection and growth, it fits the description of a Yoda.

Partnerships: Developing a partnership is a greater investment of time and money than any of the other strategies above. These are typically multi-year and involve a combination of people, programs, products, and services. The combination of the previous 3Ps with the addition of "services" sets this P apart from the others. When we think of "partnerships," we're referring to consultant-type services that generally push in for on-site support. The examples that we draw on here are the ones that we provide for schools and districts.

Connie, for example, partners with teachers to bring professional learning to the classroom. She uses the gradual release of responsibility framework to scaffold for teachers and school leaders as they learn to apply best practices into their classrooms and schools. Capacity and efficacy are fostered through small successes that lead to big results.

Joe and T.J. have an array of leadership development services, including a support for groups of teachers to develop a set of high leverage instructional strategies, called Principles of Instruction, and a professional learning experience for teachers to hone their skills in the four areas that we named above – Instructional Strategies, Content Knowledge, Grading and Assessment, and Teacher and Student Dispositions.

When you hire the right consultant to fill a need that you can't do on your own, you're making an investment that profits the whole system and targets the needs of your best teachers and possibly all of your teachers.

Maximizing Your Investment: Double Down for Teacher Leaders

Your Yoda search should be exciting, and you shouldn't feel guilty that every teacher doesn't get their own Yoda. They don't all need one. Many of your mediocre and backbone teachers just aren't there yet or could benefit from more of a skilled generalist, and their regular observation schedule will hopefully benefit in helping to make improvements to their practice. And, now that you created a physical or digital space for professional learning resources, those tools will help as well. Let's focus on developing teacher leaders. Doing so will maximize your investment in your best teachers.

If you don't already have a team of teacher leaders, that's step one. These teams are typically made up of grade level leaders, department chairs, support staff, etc. They serve as a "principal's cabinet" of sorts and work to lead initiatives, clarify expectations, run meetings, and more. We don't want to assume that you have a teacher leadership team (sometimes called an instructional leadership team or ILT) because we've helped schools and districts build these teams, even creating pots of money to pay them. That said, let's say you do have some sort of a teacher leadership team or at least a few unofficial teachers who are leaders in your school.

These folks need a focus on leadership and developing the ability to lead effectively. Too often, we find "teacher leaders" who have been put in that role and the only prerequisite was that they were great teachers, or, worse yet, the only one willing to do it. We also want to note that if your mediocre teachers are in leadership roles (official or unofficial), the school will find it difficult to flourish. In fact, the status quo will barely be maintained. It's worth saying again, as Whitaker and Gruenert first wrote in *School Culture Rewired*, "your culture is defined by the worst behaviors that the leader is willing to tolerate" (Gruenert & Whitaker, 2015). If you have mediocre teachers in leadership positions, that's the level of teaching and leading that you're willing to accept from everyone.

Back to the support that your teacher leaders need. Just because they are great teachers doesn't mean that they possess the skills to be great leaders. However, the better the teacher the more likely they have leadership skills to share. Many of the skills from teaching transfer to leadership but not all and certainly not all transfer from leading students in a classroom to leading adults in a school. That's why one of your resource sections should be about teacher leadership, books like *Every Teacher a Leader: Developing the Needed Dispositions, Knowledge, and Skills for Teacher Leadership* by Levin and Schrum (2016). And, we suggest pure leadership books as well, like *The 21 Irrefutable Laws of Leadership* by Maxwell (1991).

Beyond having a leadership section in your professional learning library, you also need to spend time during your leadership team meeting dissecting the tenets of great leadership. If 30–50% of your leadership team meeting isn't spent on learning to lead – with time used only to discuss challenges, ideas, and initiatives – then that time is mostly wasted. Leadership growth is essential to building a school that works to drive student achievement. If the people sitting around the table talking about the school's initiatives aren't equipped to lead others through the conflict that the change will inevitably cause, the work is set up for failure from the start.

Since your best teachers are often found in these settings, the leadership development they gain as a part of the team will most certainly be used in other settings. When collaborating with other teachers, they might use consensus building techniques to get their peers on board for a school change. Their mindfulness and conflict resolution skills will allow contentious conversations with parents or community members to be more productive and solution based. Doubling down on any of your best teachers' leadership skills is a good bet to make if you're trying to maximize your return on their influence in the school.

How Y.O.D.A.S. Profits the Whole System

The Y.O.D.A.S. Model profits the whole school in three distinct ways. First, the vulnerability you demonstrate as a leader – to admit that there are areas in which others are more knowledgeable – can go a long way to building trust. Second, the Yoda-level support that you provide will help your best teachers to become Yodas themselves. (Luke Skywalker did become the strongest Jedi in the system.) Third, when your best (or any) teachers become stronger leaders, their influence expands. All three of these outcomes combined improves productivity and the sense of inspiration that all teachers get from working in a school that cares this much about top performers.

Vulnerability at Work

When a leader is vulnerable in the ways that the Y.O.D.A.S. Model initiates, it permeates the entire school with a sense of psychological safety. Psychological safety is one component necessary for people to take risks. By being vulnerable about the aspects of leading teachers that you don't feel expert enough to make suggestions for your best teachers to grow, you're modeling the concept that we don't all have to know everything, that it's okay to take risks, and that you want everyone to grow more than you want everyone to see you as important or all-knowing. This has seriously positive ramifications for the overall school culture that everyone feels at work.

Yoda-Level Support

Providing Yoda-level support for your best teachers is the ideal approach to creating a team of Yodas in your school. Once you have a team of Yodas, and more teachers earn their way into the superstar category, you have Yodas to deploy without too much of a search. Remember, don't just build up your best teachers to Yoda status and then heap more work onto their shoulders. Only use your Yoda teachers when the benefit is mutual, and you'll find ample instances where this will be abundantly clear.

Stronger Teacher Leaders

Finally, we don't have to explain much about the benefits that arise when your teacher leaders become better leaders. When you have strong leaders amongst the ranks of teachers in a school, and they believe in the vision and direction that you're headed, you can expect almost infinite possibilities, including better outcomes for students. As Tom Peters (Peters & Waterman, 2006), author of *In Search of Excellence*, says, "great leaders don't create followers, they create more leaders."

 ## The Bottom Line

When you invest in your best teachers in a way that supports their growth and development, you're increasing their net worth to the school. Because our superstars have such honed and specific technical skills, we need other, more expert observers, to help add value in ways that we can be limited in providing on our own. Yes, you can successfully deliver P.E.A.C².H. feedback to teachers without having taught their subject or grade level, but when our best people exceed our own understanding of their craft, it's our responsibility to be vulnerable enough to search for outside help. Whether that support comes in the form of a person, program, product, or partner – *the 4Ps of a Yoda Search* – doesn't matter as long as your best teachers get what they need to enrich or enhance their skills.

The bottom line when you invest in your best using the Y.O.D.A.S. Model is leadership, leadership, leadership. It takes leadership to do a leadership assessment, uncovering your strengths and weaknesses. It takes leadership to admit that you have gaps in your instructional leadership, even if these gaps are only exposed with your best people because of their expert knowledge that you're lacking. It takes leadership to search for and accept help from the outside. And, it takes leadership to spend time and resources on building the capacity of your teacher leaders. If there's an important secondary takeaway from this chapter – beyond the use of the Y.O.D.A.S. Model – it's that leadership matters, and your best teachers need leadership as much as anyone else in your school.

HOW TO MAKE YOUR INITIAL DEPOSIT

The easiest first step toward using the Y.O.D.A.S. Model is to start with yourself – the Y in Y.O.D.A.S. Use the self-reflection questions to uncover the areas of instructional leadership where you're strong as well as what you should start working on. Your initial deposit doesn't have to be for someone else. Remember, when you invest in yourself, you're investing in the whole school. Like our friend Danny Bauer says: "when the leader gets better, we all win" (2018). Uncover one aspect of instructional leadership that you want to know more about and buy a book to read about it.

9

Nurturing Self- and Collective Efficacy

Lisa Grows With Praise

Lisa Dougherty was a phenomenal math teacher when she was in the classroom. She met every mark of what it means to be a "best" teacher in any school. The problem was that she didn't know it. She wasn't even remotely aware of her greatness. No one had ever told her. Maybe no one had ever noticed or understood. The nuances present in her ability to teach students were granular. She commanded the room, and she knew how to get students to apply their mathematical computation skills in a way that set them on a path to success with mathematics in her classroom and beyond. But since Lisa, like most other teachers, hadn't been in many other classrooms she really had no comparatives to get reinforced for her excellence.

Later, we would realize some of her successes when her students would not only go on to use mathematics in life, but more than a few would become math teachers. That's a testimonial that speaks for itself. But before she could realize the feedback of a student becoming a math teacher ten years after being in her classroom, she was unaware, or at least unsure, of her skills and abilities or the value that she added to both the lives of the students and the school as a community.

DOI: 10.4324/9781003321316-9

T.J. met Lisa when he was an assistant principal. She was meek-mannered, well planned, and thoroughly executed in her facilitation of her math classroom. T.J. was assigned to supervise the math department at the middle school where Lisa taught. She was there for years before he arrived. She was a conscientious teacher who did her best and brought her best-self to work each day. She had a positive attitude and a great work-ethic, but she wasn't a leader. That's where things changed.

After T.J. observed Lisa for an official teacher observation (long before walkthroughs were prevalent as an instructional leadership strategy), they sat for their post-observation conference. Lisa braced herself for the feedback. T.J. had plenty of glowing comments, explaining the specifics of Lisa's performance as well as the importance of each move she made. She was surprised, maybe even confused by the feedback. She had never heard such glowing praise for her work.

Fast forward, Lisa's self-efficacy improved that year. She went on to become the Grade Level Leader, a post that gave her access to all classrooms at her grade level with the responsibility to improve instruction. She later became the Math Specialist for the district and moved on to Math Coordinator after that. She even earned the titles of school and district teacher of the year. Her increased sense of self-efficacy came from the pride, reflection, affirmation, and praise she received. The awareness of her success and the evidence to support it ultimately gave her the confidence to move on and raise the bar for other teachers. Her future is bright, and it all started with the praise that she had never known about the impact that she has as a teacher and leader in schools.

The Costs Associated With Empty or Absent Kudos

As we come to a close with our final chapter, we want to acknowledge that there's a likelihood that you picked up this book because you know the power of investing in your best teachers. The title doesn't leave any of the content to speculation, which is by design. With that in mind, we hope that you'll think about your "best teachers" in a new light after reading this book. In fact, we hope that you'll view the entire concept of school improvement from a new lens as well. Included in your new view on how to grow, support, and celebrate your most valuable teachers should be the following:

1. *Your best teachers may receive a limited benefit by some of the growth and development practices that are used with everyone else.* Until you differentiate your approach with your best staff members in mind, you're accepting *their* status quo, albeit greater than others. Blanket professional development that we apply to a whole school hopefully helps backbone and mediocre teachers, but it may not automatically address the needs of your best staff. As long as your best teachers are not continually improving, it puts a cap on the potential of our school.

2. Unless you intentionally and explicitly say so, *there is a good chance that your best teachers may not even know that you hold them in high regard.* Letting them know why they are so effective, with evidence to support their impact, is a necessary step in supporting their growth. And, similar to how we develop plans to educate our most high achieving students, we need the same approach for our most high achieving teachers.

3. *If you invest in your best, the rest will have a chance to rise to their level of performance.* It's a simple principle of economics that "a rising tide lifts all boats." When we add value to our best people, they turn-key that value into results faster and deeper than we would with any other group. Our best teachers deserve our time and attention so that their value is known. Pockets of excellence develop into a school-wide culture of greatness where the bar is raised for the whole school.

All of that said, there's one final aspect of supporting our superstar teachers that comes at a cost if we don't do it well. If your praise for their work isn't explicitly directed toward them and their effectiveness, it's possible that they will never know what's special about them and the impact that they make on students and the school as a whole. Unfortunately, the power of praise is still underused or misunderstood in most organizations. We have found that even when leaders praise their staff, it lacks two key elements. Too often the language used to articulate what was done well is inadequate and too much time passes by between the action and the praise. As a result, we dedicate this final chapter to your use of praise as a way to elevate your best teachers in both their minds and the collective efforts of the whole school.

When we don't communicate how well our teachers are performing, they make up for the lack of communication with whatever story that is playing out in their minds. There's a big problem with this void since our brains are wired to notice negativity more than positivity (Levari, 2018). This goes back to prehistoric times when physical danger was real and present in human lives. Fast forward to the present day, when our safety is seemingly jeopardized, our bodies react before our brains even process what's going on. Perhaps this explains why when information is missing, people tend to create their own narratives about what the truth might be, often making negative assumptions. It's a survival technique.

If your mantra is "no news is good news" when it comes to supporting teachers, you might be more susceptible to allowing other people's opinions or fears to take the place of your own thoughts and beliefs as a leader. Why take the risk that your teachers will interpret your silence as disapproval? Let the following statistics speak for themselves:

- ◆ 90% of open teaching positions are created by teachers who left the profession (Carver-Thomas & Darling-Hammond, 2017).
- ◆ 82% of workers consider recognition an important part of their happiness at work (Cocchi, 2022).
- ◆ 63% of employees who are recognized are very unlikely to look for a new job (BasuMallick, 2021).
- ◆ Two-thirds of teachers leaving education voluntarily leave before retirement (Carver-Thomas & Darling-Hammond, 2017).

◆ 54% of teachers say they are somewhat or very likely to leave teaching in the next two years (Loewus, 2021).

◆ 40% of employed Americans would put energy into their work if they were recognized more often (Novak, 2016).

As long-time educators, we know that the reasons for teachers who walk away from a profession that they love are complex. However, it is undeniable that job-related stress is a factor. Leaders who fail to communicate how important their teachers are to the schools leave teachers questioning their worth to the system. This creates unnecessary stress in an already stressful job. A school leader's words potentially hold the validation that teachers need to affirm that they are needed, that they are appreciated, and that they make a difference.

Nonetheless, the truth about praise when it comes to organizational leadership is that it's practically non-existent, especially in places where morale is already low. Gostick and Elton report that 56% of people with low morale at work also claim that their boss is a failure at recognizing people for their success. They reveal that "79 percent of employees who quit their jobs cite a lack of appreciation as a key reason for leaving" (Gostick & Elton, 2009, p. 8). But the problem is deeper than celebrating and recognizing success.

The bigger issue is that when leaders are completely driven to make changes for greater success, they often miss the bright spots that can be replicated from person-to-person or program-to-program. Because leaders are pressured and expected to make positive changes, they spend so much energy on *what* to change that they often miss *how* to change. This critical omission blinds them to the incredible work that's being done right before their eyes. Worse yet, in the pursuit of change, they may also overlook some of the positive outcomes that the school is producing, a symptom of their extreme focus on the things that aren't going well.

In schools, this is problematic, not just because a lack of praise leads to low morale, but because of the missed opportunities to celebrate and lift the things that are working. The truth is that if we invest even the smallest amount of time on the best people and the most notable initiatives, the dividends are greater than working to correct and change the busted stuff. We realize that this can be challenging and may feel counterintuitive since "our focus, in times of change, goes instinctively to the problems at hand" (Heath & Heath, 2010).

When things aren't working well, leaders put their heads down and get to work. Unfortunately, while ducking down, we limit our vision. Effective school leaders know that they need to ask themselves a "…question that sounds simple but is, in fact, deeply unnatural: What's working and how can we do more of it?" (Heath & Heath, 2010). These are called "bright spots," and this type of asset-based thinking should be the focus of our time and energy because they often provide the solution that we're looking to generate.

This isn't a new concept in education; it's just underused and misunderstood. In 2003, Todd observed that one thing great principals do differently is that they base every decision on their best people. He called for a formula that included reflecting on what the best teachers would think about your decisions. The implication in doing so is the first step in recognizing bright spots, and then capitalizing on them. We have to make investments in our best people so that their impact is greater. Keeping our best people in mind as we make decisions is essential, but the true reward comes from a concentration on lifting them and expanding their greatness.

It's not just about tapping into their expertise or employing them to do more. We're talking about increasing their ability to make a difference in the classroom, ensuring that they're supported as a group of high-output individuals, and allowing them to stretch as school leaders. When school leaders harness the potential of investing in their best, they no longer have the singular worry about how they can fix problems but rather uncover a newfound strength in positioning the best teachers as a focal-point and source for solutions for the school.

So why is it that we don't praise our best people consistently and pervasively? It's not just because our focus isn't on the bright spots but because we often don't know how. From a technical standpoint, school leaders simply aren't trained on how to strengthen their best people through well-framed praise. They may lack the skills to praise effectively, or they may not fully understand the value in what praise can provide for teachers, especially the superstars. That's why we put together our P.R.A.I.S.E. Model – to provide leaders with the support to give more praise, to do it with confidence that it will work, and to understand the outcomes that it can provide.

Investment #9: Include P.R.A.I.S.E.

The first key to providing effective praise is not to always be on the lookout for something to improve but to find something that's worthy of praise. Somehow, classroom visits have been distorted into a time and space to solely improve practice versus to also use the visits as an opportunity to elevate, pinpoint, and double down on the things that are working. This is what's called deficit-thinking and it's the polar opposite of asset-based thinking, which hones in on the bright spots. Fortunately, when we're talking about our superstars, there's far more to celebrate than there is to critique. But for all teachers there are more than likely specific things you can reinforce. We call it looking for the good part even if we have to squint.

The second key to effective praise is that our language is specific. Joe and T.J. wrote about this at length in *Retention for a Change*, providing a model for leaders to follow to use praise effectively. Remember, when it's *not* done well, it doesn't show up on the receiver's radar as praise, which leaves them with a negative interpretation of your communication. The model is easy to follow:

1. Open with a praise statement;
2. Be specific about what you noticed;
3. Provide a rationale that's tied to the vision or the instructional focus of the school; and
4. Close the feedback loop by ensuring that the receiver knows it's praise (another praise statement).

> Great job with your think-pair-share today. I noticed the specific time you allocated for "thinking." Your use of a timer to monitor the silence allowed the children to spend the time needed to reflect before sharing. It's important that they get time to reflect so that the sharing of their thoughts is meaningful, which is our focus this year as a school: Student Discourse. Very nicely done, an expert model for everyone to follow. Thank you.

You can go through the sample above, using the four-part model, to identify each part. For praise to be effective, your superstars – and everyone else who you praise – need to know that you're praising them, exactly what they did to deserve it, why their actions are important, and your final words of celebration to conclude the feedback. The model is especially important in the case of written feedback, which ends up being the way we communicate to teachers because of the nature of what they're doing when we're in the room.

At face-value, you may see this practice as an opportunity to get better at celebrating your best teachers, but it's even more than that when done well. By using specific praise, we stimulate a response for them to repeat what we praise. We want our best teachers to know why they're practices are effective and elevate them as the best. This reinforces effective actions that we want repeated that leads to greater student achievement. By using praise, we can support our best teachers and help them to see what they should continue to place as the focus of their lesson plans. Praise doesn't just celebrate, it reinforces best practices.

To that end, we want to introduce you to our model for P.R.A.I.S.E. that reflects the actual outcomes that we want when we look to replicate the practices that occur within the classrooms of our best teachers. Note that each aspect of the model indicates a *description* of the practice itself, how the best teachers should *feel* when it's used, and what we want them to *do* based on it. Our hope is that you'll use this model with your best teachers so that the concept of *repeating* a practice becomes equally important to you as *improving* one.

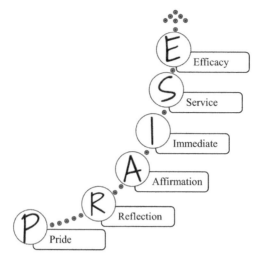

FIGURE 9.1

Our model for P.R.A.I.S.E., as shown in Figure 9.1, reflects and reinforces the actual outcomes that we want to replicate within the classrooms of our best teachers. Note that each aspect of the model indicates a description of the practice itself, how the best teachers should feel when it's used, and what we want them to do based on it. As an aside, our *describe-feel-do* sequence can be used in other scenarios where school leaders are working to replicate or scale practices. It signifies that there's a what, an emotion, and an action when we're making a change or when we're strengthening something that's done well.

Pride

Any time that we want to replicate a teacher's practice across a department, grade level, or the entire school, we should first-and-foremost instill pride in that person. Pride is an incredibly important and powerful feeling for employees who are demonstrating greatness. "In fact, pride is one of a select group of emotions that engenders perseverance and success at work" (DeSteno, 2016). Research regarding workplace pride demonstrates that a feeling of pride can build self-control and lead to grit. The outcome is a worker, in this case a teacher, who is future-forward with a strong sense that she can overcome new obstacles

(DeSteno, 2016). This has to guide leaders when we look to invest in our best people, especially when the strategy is to replicate excellent performance across the system.

Grant and Gino (2010) found that the best way to increase pride (defined as social worth) is through an expression of gratitude, especially coming from someone who doesn't typically interact with the person being valued. That's another point about finding a Yoda for your best teachers. Of course, praise has to come from supervisors, but it should also come from the fact that you've sought to find someone to observe and comment on your best teachers because no one else at the school could have done it as well as Yoda.

Reflection

One important aspect for when we make investments in our best teachers is that they have the chance to reflect on their own practice. People generally think about what they are doing when they have to teach others while they are doing it, which puts them in a reflective state and better prepares them to discuss their practices and answer questions. Even though actively reflecting on our work is a powerful practice to learn and grow, teaching is such a demanding job that most teachers don't actually have the time to reflect on their practice while they're teaching. "It's hard to think about how things are going when you're in the middle of trying to make them go well!" (Willingham, 2009, p. 193).

That said, Lanaj, Foulk, and Erez (2018) studied reflection as a daily practice for leaders. They found that those who reflected on a positive aspect of their influence for only a few minutes per day "subsequently felt less depleted and more engaged, and they reported having a positive impact on their followers." This is precisely the outcome that we want for our best teachers. The more we praise our best teachers to show them how valuable they are, the more of a positive influence that they will have on everyone else.

Affirmation

We can never take for granted the incredible work being done by our most successful teachers. The best educators on staff should be affirmed and know the impact that their work has on students and colleagues. The interesting thing is that our most motivated and strongest performers are also the most hesitant about whether or not they're doing well (Gostic & Elton, 2007). Affirmation reinforces their expertise and lets them know how much they are appreciated. When they don't feel valued, they're not sure about their performance, which can lead to attrition.

Schwantes (2017) says that one way to mitigate the lack of security at work is to affirm their future and ask if we can learn from them. Expressing the need for others to learn from our best people is what affirms that they're doing well and that we want them to stay on the team. It's why affirmation is a critical aspect of our P.R.A.I.S.E. Model and a result of our R.O.L.E. Play strategy from Chapter 6. Nonetheless, praising our best teachers solidifies their position on the team and affirms that we want their future to be with us at this school.

Immediate

Any strategy that strives to instill pride in a teacher or affirm their work should also be timely. Similar to a student receiving prompt feedback on an assignment, we should give teachers prompt feedback. The goal is that whatever strategy we use for feedback occurs as close to the work they're doing as practically possible. In other words, providing praise should happen while teachers are teaching or shortly thereafter. The praise shouldn't be random or days later. As Blanchard and Bowles (1998) described in *Gung Ho!*, true congratulations for a job well done needs to be timely.

We applaud leaders who use regular celebrations, including the highlights that some leaders publish in their weekly newsletters. But, nothing communicates gratitude better than a personal compliment or commendation *as* people are doing the work. When observing teachers for informal visits, don't leave the room without hitting "send" on your feedback. Your best teachers want to know what you think more than anyone else. They deserve to know in real time or as close to it as you can come.

Service

"Giving back increases self-esteem. Knowing that you're doing your part in helping others makes you feel good about yourself, and that's something no one can take away from you" (Edwards, 2018). It's important for our best teachers to have an avenue to impact the school beyond that of their general duties as instructors. Medical doctor Barbara Edwards says that service doesn't just provide self-fulfillment, it allows people to become more aware of the world around them. Service to the greater community in a school gives our best teachers a stronger sense of purpose and helps them contribute to the profession as they work with other educators.

This is a different level of satisfaction that we want our superstars to feel as often as possible. It means that when you give praise, you should note how the specific action of your teacher impacted the whole school and the overall goals of the school. It also means that we should regularly conference with our best people annually to ask them about the impact that they would like to have on the school that can go beyond their regular job description. Leaders who do this well find release time for their best teachers to have an impact that transcends what they do daily with their own group of students.

Efficacy

The final element of our P.R.A.I.S.E. Model is our ability to instill a belief within our teachers that they have the capacity to positively impact their students. This belief is a social construct called self-efficacy. According to Bandura (1986), there are four influencers in self-efficacy, and they are ranked in order of their impact. First is mastery experiences. When teachers achieve success and that success is a result of conditions they control, it fuels their belief that these results can be duplicated. The next factor in self-efficacy is vicarious experiences. Teachers who are exposed to others' successes through site visits, observation, case studies, and other formats can build a thought process that "If they can do it, we can do it too." The third component is social persuasion. Teams of educators can positively influence the individuals within the team through persuasion. The fourth and final source of self-efficacy is emotional states. This is described by Donohoo as "feelings of excitement or anxiety associated with an individual's perceptions of his or her capability or incompetence" (Donohoo, 2017, p. 8).

Our best teachers are integral players in bringing these sources of efficacy to the culture of the school. The greater the degree of self-efficacy, the more likely we'll work toward a collective efficacy. When our best teachers know and understand their effectiveness, they make it possible, through Bandura's four influences, for others to feel the same. The result is a better working environment for everyone to tackle any challenge. That said, praise is a key component so our best teachers know and understand their effectiveness, which calls attention to the successful experiences that they're providing for their students. The more aware they are of their own positive impact on student learning, the more their self-efficacy grows and influences the collective good.

Our P.R.A.I.S.E. Model, along with the research and philosophy behind it, is designed to create success as you work to invest in your best people. It allows the user to take a deep breath, restrain from the constant critical analysis of what they can improve, and focus on what should be repeated and even replicated across the school. The more we champion our best teachers to solidify what works in the classroom, over-and-over, the better they are positioned to act as a guide for others to do the same, as we have shared throughout the book.

Maximizing Your Investment: Understand the Psychology of Praise

If there's a phrase that we would like to go down in history as saying often, it's this one: *Leadership is as much about psychology as it is about anything else.* The reality is that once you leave the classroom to become a coach or supervisor, you cannot be an expert in everything. However, leaders need to be experts in giving and receiving feedback. In Chapter 7, we introduced you to the P.E.A.C².H. Model for providing feedback. In this chapter we look at the impact that the power of praise makes, which is a specific type of feedback. Once you realize that feedback is a separate skill that every form of problem solving and improvement strategy is communicated through, you understand that nothing improves without a culture built on it.

The problem is that leaders are rarely trained on *how* feedback, including the way we praise, works to effectively improve performance and the psychological benefits of feedback. In fact, at best, they took a supervision course that touched on it. When we talk about feedback in education, we usually refer to rubrics and tools on student assignments rather than the culture of the school. The strategy to maximize your investment we can give you is to recognize that feedback drives performance. Whether you read about it, take a Masterclass, or subscribe to business magazines that dwell on it, feedback is a skill that must be mastered.

The point is that coaches and supervisors, anyone who observes teachers, need to be well versed in the behavior and organizational psychology regarding praise as a form of feedback. To support that effort, we offer the following concepts as a starting place for your basic understanding of how feedback triggers (or doesn't) a positive response.

1. The first concept is called "the illusion of transparency." Studies have indicated that feedback providers are far more confident that what they said was clear to the receiver than it actually was and that receivers perceive feedback as more positive than the provider meant it to be. In other words, when the feedback provider wanted to deliver constructive criticism, it ended up being unintentionally inflated or sugar coated during delivery (Schaerer & Swaab, 2019). And, when we think we're praising people for their work, they may not interpret what we're saying as praise.

    The number one way to overcome this problem is to give feedback more frequently in an environment that acknowledges the power of it. Since feedback is challenging, whether it's correcting something or praising something, it's important to send the messages as often and as timely as you can. "Research has found that giving feedback more frequently makes feedback more accurate" (Schaerer & Swaab, 2019).

2. The second concept is the negative bias of "The Velcro/ Teflon Phenomenon." Simply put, it's "our tendency to remember the bad and forget or dismiss the good" (Chandler, 2019, p. 41). Those of us who give feedback by the nature of our jobs have to remember that it's a basic human instinct to focus on the bad or negative feedback we receive. It's a survival technique.

    When critical feedback arises, we learn from it, and remember it, so that we don't do whatever prompted it again. The good part about this is that it further demonstrates how feedback is essential to improvement, but it also shows that we can become immune to positive feedback when our brains are acting like velcro regarding any negative feedback. This means that our praise should be a focal point more often, it builds toward our final concept.

3. The final concept is simple, and it overlaps with the themes from this chapter. Here it is: you can't praise people often enough. The psychological barrier that leaders need to understand if they want to be effective at providing feedback is that they likely undervalue the impact of praise. Zenger and Folkman (2017) found that many leaders "vastly underestimate the power and necessity of positive reinforcement." Worse yet, the same study found that leaders also "overestimate the value and benefit of negative or corrective feedback."

    It means that leaders are focused on what they can improve versus what they should emphasize. Unfortunately, too many leaders believe that providing praise makes them look weak (Zenger & Folkman, 2017). Not only is this untrue, it creates a major missed opportunity to support the people who are doing great work. When we understand this barrier, it helps us to realize that we can't use praise enough, especially with our best people.

In terms of the literature on feedback and the psychology of giving and receiving it, we're just scratching the surface here. We're making the case that leaders need to be well versed in how feedback may or may not elicit an emotional response, depending on how the feedback is crafted. That said, the first step to improving the frequency and quality of your feedback, and improving the level at which it is accepted in the culture of your school, is to start with praise. The more praise we give, the greater our entry-way into providing constructive feedback that won't stick to the velcro brains of those who fear it. This is important for our best teachers, but as we work toward becoming feedback experts, our newfound understanding will help to lift the whole school.

🔒 How P.R.A.I.S.E. Profits the Whole System

In Dewitt's 2022 book called *Collective Leader Efficacy*, he pointed out that "many ILTs [Instructional Leadership Teams] do not reach their potential of impacting student learning because they don't see themselves as the drivers of improvement…" (p. 13). Unfortunately, when they don't see themselves as drivers of improvement – student improvement, teacher improvement, and school improvement – very little will change. Why don't our teachers, even our best teachers (who often serve on the ILTs), see themselves as change agents?

One reason is that many schools still accept and maintain the status quo. We should say *their* status quo because every school's status quo is different. And, the main reason for that is because they don't feel like they have the power to change anything. That's Bandura's basic definition of self-efficacy, or lack thereof. "Self-efficacy refers to beliefs in one's capabilities to organize and execute the courses of action required to produce given attainments" (Bandura, 1997, p. 3). In other words, teachers and school leaders lack the self-efficacy to implement improvement strategies. They may even know the strategies to use but don't feel effective in using them.

The good news is that Bandura (1997) also uncovered four ways in which we can strengthen self-efficacy: 1. Mastery experiences, 2. Vicarious experiences, 3. Social persuasion, and 4. Affective states. Our P.R.A.I.S.E. Model combines a number of these experiences to help build the self-efficacy of our best teachers. If our best teachers don't have self-efficacy, everyone else is practically doomed. And, we haven't found literature that supports the existence of an environment where collective efficacy is high and self-efficacy is low. This ties back to our E in the P.R.A.I.S.E. Model; the more we apply the model with our superstars, the higher their degree of self-efficacy.

To push the conversation further as to why our best teachers' self-efficacy is so important, we point to two outcomes. The first is that when the self-efficacy of our best teachers is high, they will see themselves as agents of change. The theory of action is that our best teachers' levels of self-efficacy are tied to their feelings of empowerment for making the rest of the school a better place to work and learn. That means that when they have mastery experiences through the use of P.R.A.I.S.E. their efficacy increases and so does their impact on the rest of the school community.

The second outcome of higher levels of self-efficacy among our best teachers is that it has a greater chance of improving whole-school collective efficacy. "Teachers work within a complex social organization. Within schools, students, teachers and administrators develop relationships that affect the organizational structure and culture" (Pierce, 2019). When our best teachers experience greater degrees of self-efficacy through the P.R.A.I.S.E. Model, their efficacy spreads within the organizational social structures to create new levels of collective efficacy among staff who might not have otherwise come to the realization that there are bright spots among staff. "Collective teacher efficacy develops based on a collective analysis of the teaching and learning environment and the assessment of the faculty's teaching competence" (Pierce, 2019). When the best teachers' work is more distinguished because of P.R.A.I.S.E., whole staff perceptions of competency goes up and so does the "I can do that too" factor associated with self-efficacy and, hence, collective efficacy.

The Bottom Line

There are several points to underscore as we conclude this chapter as the final of the nine strategies to grow, support, and celebrate your most valuable teachers. The first is that regardless of your observational skills as an instructional leader, you can hone your skills with feedback, especially with providing praise. When you know the costs of not praising, you understand the reasons for doing, and you practice the skills of doing it well (using our four-part model), you learn to do it more often.

The second point is that our P.R.A.I.S.E. Model brings out the best in your most effective teachers. They should feel pride from the gratitude that you frequently express; they should have opportunities to reflect on their impact at the school level; we should affirm their position on the team as secure and important; their praise should be immediate; and any other service that they wish to provide should be honored. Using P.R.A.I.S.E. with your superstars will drive the culture for everyone else.

Our P.R.A.I.S.E. Model focuses on building the self-efficacy of our best teachers so that they see themselves as agents of change for school improvement and so that they contribute to the collective efficacy of the whole school community. The model lifts the systems by elevating from the top versus the models of the past where leaders find themselves pushing from the bottom, focusing on the mediocre teachers and ignoring the best ones. You can change that in your school starting today to ensure that your best teachers are lifted as leaders like what happened with Lisa.

One final point when it comes to praise. Whenever you praise, at least two people feel better and one of them is you. Realize that investing in the best means that if we do it correctly, everyone can benefit...including you. We have to treat people special because they are special. And the more we treat people in this fashion the more likely they are to reach this standard. Leaders who focus on the best become the best. Thank you for working to have a positive impact. It makes a difference.

HOW TO MAKE YOUR INITIAL DEPOSIT

To reap the benefits of the P.R.A.I.S.E. Model and to build collective teacher efficacy at your school, you can start small. Jot down one or two aspects of teaching and learning that you want every teacher to get good at. We already know that our best teachers are likely to be the best at these things. Go back to the four-part P.R.A.I.S.E. Model at the beginning of the Investment section of this chapter. Review all four parts of the model. Use the model to reinforce the one or two aspects of teaching and learning that you jotted down. You can start by using the model to praise and celebrate your best teachers, but it doesn't stop there. Try to praise as many teachers as possible this week. Make sure to use all four parts of the model. It's easy, fun, and makes a difference for your teachers' sense of pride and belonging in the school.

Conclusion

Our drive to write this book was to encourage school and district leaders to focus on what's working in their schools – to identify, magnify, and replicate the bright spots within each school and district so that they can serve as a blueprint for other educators with an opportunity to extend their shine and brighten the path for everyone. As challenges surface, the investments we've made will pay off because when energy is dedicated to asset-based thinking, where leadership and staff alike leverage strengths, collective efficacy and a can-do attitude, we have no doubt, will lead to sustaining solutions to any problem – even the perennial ones.

This tightly held belief and philosophy initially propelled Connie, Joe, and T.J. to author *7 Mindshifts for School Leaders: Finding New Ways to Think About Old Problems* (2023). The entire book is focused on lingering problems in education and guiding leaders to think about them differently so that meaningful solutions arise. *Invest in Your Best* is also a new way of thinking about how to lift and improve a system. We know that by identifying, understanding, and celebrating the bright spots, especially the teachers, elevates everyone, not just the best teachers. Systems are lifted by replicating and duplicating the efforts, skills, and attitudes that create success.

A core tenet of problem solving is to ensure that the right people are at the table, willing to work through the most challenging of circumstances. Elevating our best work and our best people creates this environment. Imagine if the majority of our efforts were focused on highlighting our best work and our most valuable people. Not only would we, as leaders, engage our time in more positivity, but our staff would feel the encouraging vibe that we share when showing appreciation, supporting teacher growth, and celebrating the school and district's successes.

DOI: 10.4324/9781003275046-10

This isn't to say that concerns or issues should be ignored or avoided, just the opposite. We believe in confronting and changing what is not working. Todd is the author of *Dealing with Difficult Teachers* (Whitaker, 2015), which addresses some of the more challenging people and situations in our schools. By directly addressing areas that can pull our best teachers down, we foster an environment where they can flourish. We care deeply about continuous improvement and tackling the areas of schooling that need attention.

We know first-hand the incredible work being done in our schools. We hope that you'll join us on a path forward that invests in our most valuable people in a way that profits the whole system. We've seen it work, and you will too. Nothing feels better than to uncover, point out, and share the outcomes of the people who are making a difference in our schools. In the end, kids benefit, and that's why we do what we do in the first place.

These investments are paramount to your success as a school leader, whether you're a teacher who wants to lift your peers or a principal who wants to change the culture or a district official who wants to tell a new story about the value of the system. They won't just motivate, inspire, and energize your staff, like Joe and T.J. shared about in *Retention for a Change* (a book about how to retain teachers), Connie wrote with Dorothy Vanderjagt about in *Strained and Drained: Tools for Overworked Teachers*, and Todd affirms in *Shifting the Monkey*, these investments are meant to enhance all educators. As we've noted throughout this book, the moment you raise excitement about the best accomplishments in the school, you boost everyone else along the way.

As we wrap up with a few closing words, we want you to feel motivated to make these investments and take the first steps that you found in our Initial Deposit sections. These strategies are empowering for your superstar teachers, but many of them can simply be used with all teachers – everyone in the school. After all, the best leaders treat people not as they currently are but as the best version of themselves given the potential that they see in them. We hope that you're better positioned to recognize your bright spots, invest in your best people, and notice the possibilities we have to grow, support, and celebrate *every* teacher.

References

Accenture. (2020). *Developing Talent in the New*. https://youtu.be/bvI1gE9GPHA

Acharya, S., & Shukla, S. (2012). Mirror neurons: Enigma of the metaphysical modular brain. *Journal of Natural Science, Biology, and Medicine, 3*(2), 118–124. https://doi.org/10.4103/0976-9668.101878

Agarwal, P. K., & Bain, P. M. (2019). *Powerful teaching: Unleash the science of learning*. Jossey-Bass.

American Psychological Association. (2012, March 8). APA survey finds feeling valued at work linked to well-being and performance [Press release]. https://www.apa.org/news/press/releases/2012/03/well-being

American Psychological Association. (2022). Education and socioeconomic status. https://www.apa.org/pi/ses/resources/publications/factsheet-education.pdf

Anjinomoto. (2022). What is umami? https://www.ajinomoto.com/umami/5-facts

Aronson, E., Stephan, C., Sikes, J., Blaney, N., & Snapp, M. (1978). *The jigsaw classroom*. Sage Publications.

Auxier, B. (2020). Pew Research Center. 64% of Americans say social media have a mostly negative effect on the way things are going in the U.S. today. https://www.pewresearch.org/fact-tank/2020/10/15/64-of-americans-say-social-media-have-a-mostly-negative-effect-on-the-way-things-are-going-in-the-u-s-today/

Bandura, A. (1986). *Social foundations of thought and action: A social cognitive theory*. Prentice-Hall.

Bandura, A. (1997). *Self-efficacy: The exercise of control*. Freeman.

Barnes, M., & Gonzalez, J. (2015). *Hacking education: 10 quick fixes for every school*. Times 10 Publication.

BasuMallick, C. (2021). 6 statistics that confirm employee recognition and retention are related. Spiceworks. https://www.spiceworks.com/hr/engagement-retention/articles/employee-recognition-and-retention-statistics/

Bauer, D. (2018). *The better leaders better schools roadmap: Small ideas that lead to big impact.* Corwin.

Bergen, A. (2013). Self-efficacy, special education students, and achievement: Shifting the lens. *Insight: Rivire Academic Journal, 9*(2), 1–9.

Blanchard, K., & Bowles, S. (1998). *Gung ho! Turn on the people in any organization.* Henry Holt and Company, Inc.

Brown, P. C. (2014). *Make it stick: The science of successful learning.* Harvard University Press.

Burchard, B. (2017). *High performance habits: How extraordinary people become that way.* Hay House.

Carroll, L. (1893). *Alice's adventures in Wonderland.* Macmillan.

Carver-Thomas, D., & Darling-Hammond, L. (2017). *Teacher turnover: Why it matters and what we can do about it.* Learning Policy Institute. https://doi.org/10.54300/454.278

Casas, J. (2017). *Culturize: Every student. Every day. Whatever it takes.* Dave Burgess Consulting, Inc.

Chandler, M. T. (2019). *Feedback (and other dirty words): Why we fear it, how to fix it.* Berrett-Koehler Publishing, Inc.

Chapman, G. D., & White, P. E. (2012). *The 5 languages of appreciation in the workplace: Empowering organizations by encouraging people* (revised and updated). Northfield Publishing.

Chappuis, J., & Stiggins, R. J. (2017). *An introduction to student-involved assessment for learning* (7th ed.). Pearson Education.

Clear, J. (2018). *Atomic habits.* Penguin Random House.

Cocchi, R. (2022). *Boost employee retention with these 8 strategies.* HRM Insider.

Cohn, J., & Rangan, U. (2020). Why CEOs should model vulnerability. *Harvard Business Review.* https://hbr.org/2020/05/why-ceos-should-model-vulnerability

Collins, J. (2001). *Good to great: Why some companies make the leap and others don't.* HarperCollins.

Cook, C. R., Grady, E. A., Long, A. C., Renshaw, T., Codding, R. S., Fiat, A., & Larson, M. (2017). Evaluating the impact of increasing general education teachers' ratio of positive-to-negative interactions on students' classroom behavior. *Journal of Positive Behavior Interventions, 19*(2), 67–77. https://doi.org/10.1177/1098300716679137

Cordovani, L., & Cordovani, D. (2016). A literature review on observational learning for medical motor skills and anesthesia teaching. *Advances in Health Science Education, 21*, 1113–1121. https://doi.org/10.1007/s10459-015-9646-5

Costa, A. L., & Garmstom, R. J. (2016). *Cognitive coaching: Developing self-directed leaders and learners*. Rowman & Littlefield.

Danielson Group. (2022a). *Our history*. https://danielsongroup.org/our-story/#:~:text=The%20Danielson%20Group%20published%20the,country%27s%2020%20largest%20school%20districts

Danielson Group. (2022b). *The Framework for Teaching*. https://danielsongroup.org/the-framework-for-teaching/

Darling-Hammond, L., Hyler, M. E., & Gardner, M. (2017). *Effective teacher professional development*. Learning Policy Institute. https://learningpolicyinstitute.org/product/effective-teacher-professional-development-report

DeSteno, D. (2016). The connection between pride and persistence. *Harvard Business Review*. https://hbr.org/2016/08/the-connection-between-pride-and-persistence

Dewitt, P. (2022). *Collective leader efficacy: Strengthening instructional leadership teams*. Corwin.

Donohoo, J. (2017). *Collective efficacy: How educators' beliefs impact student learning*. Corwin.

Donohoo, J., & Katz, S. (2017). The learning professional. *When Teachers Believe, Students Achieve, 38*(6). https://learningforward.org/wp-content/uploads/2017/12/when-teachers-believe-students-achieve.pdf

Du Maurier, G. (1894). *Trilby: A novel*. Lulu.

Dynarski, M. (2016, December 8). Teacher observations have been a waste of time and money. Brookings. https://www.brookings.edu/research/teacher-observations-have-been-a-waste-of-time-and-money/

Educator Effectiveness. (n.d.). https://www.mischooldata.org/educator-effectiveness/

Edwards, B. R. (2018). Why being of service improves happiness.. *PsychCentral*. https://psychcentral.com/blog/why-being-of-service-improves-happiness/

Feldman, J. (2018). *Grading for equity: What it is, why it matters, and how it can transform schools and classrooms*. Corwin.

Flywheel Effect. (n.d.). https://www.jimcollins.com/concepts/the-flywheel.html

Frei, F. X., & Morriss, A. (2020, May). Begin With Trust. *Harvard Business Review*.

Friedman, T. L. (2005). *The world is flat: A brief history of the twenty-first century*. Farrar, Straus and Giroux.

Futernick, K. (2007). *A possible dream: Retaining California teachers so all students learn*. California State University.

Gallo, A. (2011). Making sure your employees succeed. *Harvard Business Review*. https://hbr.org/2011/02/making-sure-your-employees-suc

Gallup. (2016). *First, break all the rules: What the world's greatest managers do differently*. Gallup Press.

Gimbert, B., Bol, L., & Wallace, D. (2007). The influence of teacher preparation on student achievement and the application of national standards by teachers of mathematics in urban secondary schools. *Education and Urban Society*, *40*, 91–117.

Gostick, A., & Elton, C. (2009). *The carrot principle: How the best managers use recognition to engage their people, retain talent, and accelerate performance*. Simon & Schuster, Inc.

Grant, A. M., & Gino, F. (2010). A little thanks goes a long way: Explaining why gratitude expressions motivate prosocial behavior. *Journal of Personality and Social Psychology*, *98*(6), 946–955.

Gruenert, S., & Whitaker, T. (2015). *School culture rewired: How to define, assess, and transform it*. ASCD.

Guskey, T. (2019). *What we know about grading: What works, what doesn't, and what's next*. ASCD.

Hamilton, C. (2017). Are you speaking your teachers' appreciation language? *We Are Teachers*. https://www.weareteachers.com/speaking-teachers-appreciation-language/

Hamilton, C. (2019). *Hacking questions: 11 answers that create a culture of inquiry in your classroom*. Times 10 Publications.

Hamilton, C., Jones, J., & Vari, T. (2023). *7 mindshifts for school leaders: Finding new ways to think about old problems*. Corwin.

Hamilton, C., and VanderJagt, D. (2022). *Strained and drained: Tools for overworked teachers*. Rowman & Littlefield.

Hargreaves, A., & Shirley, D. (2009). *The fourth way: The inspiring future for educational change*. Corwin Press.

Harvard GSE (n.d.). Data wise: Using collaborative data inquiry to build equitable schools. https://www.gse.harvard.edu/ppe/program/data-wise-using-collaborative-data-inquiry-build-equitable-schools

Hattie, J. (2008). *Visible learning: A synthesis of over 800 meta-analyses relating to achievement*. Routledge.

Hattie, J. (2012). *Visible learning for teachers: Maximizing impact on learning*. Routledge.

Hattie, J. (2021, August). Visible learning – Meta X. https://www.visiblelearningmetax.com/

Heath, D., & Heath, C. (2010). Switch: Don't solve problems – copy success. *Fast Company*. https://www.fastcompany.com/90455933/how-design-can-stop-the-spread-of-the-wuhan-coronovirus

Hunter, S., & Springer, M. G. (2022). Critical feedback characteristics, teacher human capital, and early-career teacher performance: A mixed-methods analysis. *Educational Evaluation and Policy Analysis*, 44(3), 380–403. https://doi.org/10.3102/01623737211062913

Izuma, K., Saito, D. N., & Sadato, N. (2008). Processing of social and monetary rewards in the human. *Striatum Neuron*, 58(2), 284–294.

Jones, J., Thomas-EL., S., & Vari, T. (2021). *Retention for a change: Motivate, inspire, and energize your school culture*. Rowman & Littlefield.

Jones, J., Thomas-EL, S., & Vari, T. (2020). *Building a winning team: The power of a magnetic reputation and the need to recruit top talent in every school*. Rowman & Littlefield.

Jones, J., & Vari, T. (2019). *Candid and compassionate feedback: Transforming everyday practice in schools*. Routledge.

Juárez Olguín, H., Calderón Guzmán, D., Hernández García, E., & Barragán Mejía, G. (2015, December 6). The role of dopamine and its dysfunction as a consequence of oxidative stress. https://www.hindawi.com/journals/omcl/2016/9730467/

Keller, G., & Papasan, J. (2012). *The ONE thing: The surprisingly simple truth about extraordinary results*. Bard Press.

Kim, J., & Choi, K. (2022). *From Chaos to Transformation: New Challenges Demanding New Approaches. District Management Journal*. https://www.dmgroupk12.com/writable/documents/DMJ31_Feature_Spotlight.pdf

Lanaj, K., Foulk, T., & Erez, A. (2018). How self-reflection can help leaders stay motivated. *Harvard Business Review*. https://hbr.org/2018/09/how-self-reflection-can-help-leaders-stay-motivated

Levari, D. (2018). Why your brain never runs out of problems to find. *The Conversation.* https://theconversation.com/why-your-brain-never-runs-out-of-problems-to-find-98990

Levin, B., & Schrum, L. (2016). *Every teacher a leader: Developing the needed dispositions, knowledge, and skills for teacher leadership.* Corwin.

LIFE Magazine. (1958, March 24). http://www.originallifemagazines.com/LIFE-Magazine-March-24-1958-P2616.aspx

Llopis, G. (2013). 6 ways effective listening can make you a better leader. *Forbes.* https://www.forbes.com/sites/glennllopis/2013/05/20/6-effective-ways-listening-can-make-you-a-better-leader/?sh=1b990e891756

Loewus, L. (2021). Why teachers leave – or don't: A look at the numbers. *Education Week.* https://www.edweek.org/teaching-learning/why-teachers-leave-or-dont-a-look-at-the-numbers/2021/05

Losada, M., & Heaphy, E. (2004). The role of positivity and connectivity in the performance of business teams. *American Behavioral Scientist, 47*(6), 740–765. doi: 10.1177/0002764203260208

Makinson, R. (2021, August 5). 6 ways micromanagement could be negatively affecting your employees. *CEO Today.* https://www.ceotodaymagazine.com/2021/08/6-ways-micromanagement-could-be-negatively-affecting-your-employees/

Marken, S., & Agrawal, S. (2022). K-12 workers have highest burnout rate in U.S. *Gallup.* https://news.gallup.com/poll/393500/workers-highest-burnout-rate.aspx

Marzano, R. J., (2007). *The art and science of teaching: A comprehensive framework for effective instruction.* Association for Supervision and Curriculum Development.

Marzano, R., Pickering, D., & Pollock, J. (2001). *Classroom instruction that works: Research-based strategies for increasing student achievement.* ASCD.

Mathur, K. (2019). How to manage teams when you're not the subject matter expert. Fast Company. https://www.fastcompany.com/90434738/how-to-manage-teams-when-youre-not-the-subject-matter-expert

Mauborgne, R., & Kim, W. C. (2017). *Blue ocean shift: Beyond competing – Proven steps to inspire confidence and seize new growth.* Hachette Books.

Maxwell, J. (1991). *The 21 irrefutable laws of leadership.* HarperCollins.

McGuffey, J., & Gustafson, K. (2019). Opinion: Trust teachers with school reform ideas. *The Detroit News.* https://www.detroitnews.com/story/opinion/2019/08/22/opinion-trust-teachers-school-reform/2083651001/

Medina, J. (2015). *Brain rules: 12 principles for surviving and thriving at work, home, and school.* Pear Press.

Miltra, D. L. (2008). Amplifying student voice. *Educational Leadership, 66*(3), 20–25.

Mitchell, H. (2021). How a side hustle can boost performance at your regular job. *The Wall Street Journal.* https://www.wsj.com/articles/how-a-side-hustle-can-boost-your-job-performance-11635533208

Novak, D. (2016). Recognizing employees is the simplest way to improve morale. *Harvard Business Review.* https://hbr.org/2016/05/recognizing-employees-is-the-simplest-way-to-improve-morale

Oakland University. (2021). Galileo Institute for Teacher Leadership. https://oakland.edu/galileo/

O'Flaherty, S., Sanders, M. T., & Whillans, A. (2021, September 17). Research: A little recognition can provide a big morale boost. *Harvard Business Review.* https://hbr.org/2021/03/research-a-little-recognition-can-provide-a-big-morale-boost

Peetz, C. (2022, November 15). The status of the teaching profession is at a 50-year low. What can we do about it? *Education Week.* https://www.edweek.org/teaching-learning/the-status-of-the-teaching-profession-is-at-a-50-year-low-what-can-we-do-about-it/2022/11#:~:text=The%20number%20of%20new%20entrants,2006%20to%20215%2C000%20in%202020

Peters, T. J., & Waterman, R. H. (2006). *In search of excellence: Lessons from America's best-run companies.* Harper Business.

Pierce, S. (2019, September/October). The importance of building collective teacher efficacy. *Leadership Magazine.* https://leadership.acsa.org/building-teacher-efficacy#:~:text=Collective%20teacher%20efficacy%20is%20an,%E2%80%9D%20(Goddard%2C%202003)%20

Prado Tuma, A., Hamilton, L., & Berglund, T., (2018). How do teachers perceive feedback and evaluation systems? rand.org. https://www.rand.org/pubs/research_briefs/RB10023.html#:~:text=Teachers%20are%20more%20likely%20to,be%20supported%20by%20school%20resources

Rabha, M. (2023, September 13). Empower the workforce with a culture of peer-to-peer recognition. Vantage Circle HR blog. https://blog.vantagecircle.com/peer-to-peer-recognition/

Sackstein, S. (2015). *Hacking assessment: 10 ways to go gradeless in a traditional grades school.* Times 10 Publishing.

Sackstein, S. (2021). *Assessing with respect: Everyday practices that meet students' social and emotional needs*. ASCD.

Schaerer, M., & Swaab, R. (2019). Are you sugarcoating your feedback without realizing it? *Harvard Business Review*. https://hbr.org/2019/10/are-you-sugarcoating-your-feedback-without-realizing-it

Schwantes, M. (2017). 9 phrases bosses should say often to inspire and motivate others. Inc.com. https://www.inc.com/marcel-schwantes/9-phrases-bosses-should-say-often-to-inspire-motivate-others.html

Schwartz,T.(2012,July23).Whyappreciationmatterssomuch.*HarvardBusiness Review*. https://hbr.org/2012/01/why-appreciation-matters-so-mu

Sheninger, E., & Rubin, T. (2017). *BrandED: Tell your story, build relationships, and empower learning*. Jossey-Bass.

Shpancer, N. (2010, August 10). What doesn't kill you makes you weaker. *Psychology Today*. https://www.psychologytoday.com/intl/blog/insight-therapy/201008/what-doesnt-kill-you-makes-you-weaker

Sinanis, T., & Sanfelippo, J. (2015). *The power of branding: Telling your school's story*. Corwin.

Skipper, C. (2018). Why your brain is wired for pessimism – And what you can do to fix it. *Gentlemen's Quarterly*. https://www.gq.com/story/how-to-be-more-optimistic

Sousa, D. (2006). *How the brain learns* (3rd ed.). Corwin Press.

Teachers Observing Teachers: A Professional Development Tool for Every School: Education World. (n.d.). https://www.educationworld.com/a_admin/admin/admin297.shtml

United States Geological Survey. (n.d.). Ninety percent of an iceberg is below the waterline. https://www.usgs.gov/media/images/ninety-percent-iceberg-below-waterline

University of Pennsylvania GSE. (2022). Project-Based Learning Certificate Program. https://www.gse.upenn.edu/academics/center-professional-learning/project-based-learning-certificate

Webb, N. L. (2002). Depth-of-knowledge for four content areas. http://ossucurr.pbworks.com/w/file/fetch/49691156/Norm%20web%20dok%20by%20subject%20area.pdf

Wei, R. C., Darling-Hammond, L., Andree, A., Richardson, N., & Orphanos, S. (2009). *Professional learning in the learning profession: A status report on teacher development in the U.S. and abroad*. Technical Report. National Staff Development Council.

Whitaker, T. (2014). *Shifting the monkey: The art of protecting good people from liars, criers, and other slackers*. Solution Tree.

Whitaker, T. (2015). *Dealing with difficult teachers*. Eye on Education.

Whitaker, T. (2020). *What great principals do differently: Twenty things that matter most*. Eye on Education.

Wiggins, G. (2012). 7 keys to effective feedback. *Educational Leadership, 70*(1), 10–16.

Wiggins, G. (2015). Taking a closer look at teacher effectiveness ratings: Part 1. TeachThought. https://www.teachthought.com/pedagogy/taking-a-closer-look-at-teacher-effectiveness-ratings-part-1/#:~:text=95.6%20percent%20of%20teachers%20were,of%20teachers%20were%20rated%20Ineffective

Willingham, D. T. (2009). *Why don't students like school?* Jossey-Bass.

Wooden, J., & Carty, J. (2005). *Coach Wooden's pyramid of success playbook: Applying the pyramid of success to your life*. Revell.

Zenger, J., & Folkman, J. (2017). Why do so many managers avoid giving praise? *Harvard Business Review*. https://hbr.org/2017/05/why-do-so-many-managers-avoid-giving-praise